JESUS EXPLAINED

JESUS EXPLAINED

QUESTIONS AND ANSWERS

JOSEPH DORÉ

TRANSLATED BY Lawrence B. Terrien

Paulist Press
New York / Mahwah, NJ

Cover image by Jozef Klopacka / Shutterstock.com
Cover design by Joe Gallagher
Book design by Lynn Else

Library of Congress Cataloging-in-Publication Data
Names: Doré, Joseph, author.
Title: Jesus explained : questions and answers / Joseph Doré ; translated by Lawrence B. Terrien.
Other titles: Jésus expliqué à tous. English
Description: New York : Paulist Press, 2020. | Summary: "Questions and answers about Jesus in four categories: history, message, identity, posterity"—Provided by publisher.
Identifiers: LCCN 2019024208 (print) | LCCN 2019024209 (ebook) | ISBN 9780809154418 (paperback) | ISBN 9781587688348 (ebook)
Subjects: LCSH: Jesus Christ.
Classification: LCC BT203 .D67413 2020 (print) | LCC BT203 (ebook) | DDC 232—dc23
LC record available at https://lccn.loc.gov/2019024208
LC ebook record available at https://lccn.loc.gov/2019024209

ISBN 978-0-8091-5441-8 (paperback)
ISBN 978-1-58768-834-8 (e-book)

Published by Paulist Press
997 Macarthur Boulevard
Mahwah, New Jersey 07430
www.paulistpress.com

Printed and bound in the
United States of America

CONTENTS

PREFACE

This book is simply intended to explain Jesus, and not only *to explain* Jesus, but to explain him *to everyone*!

For anyone who wishes to set out on this journey and who already has an idea of what it is all about, we will begin by pointing out some fundamental elements that will need to be confirmed in what follows.

It is more than twenty centuries since the birth of a man named Jesus[1] in what was then called Palestine (more or less the "Israel" of today). His words and his actions aroused the interest of many people; then a certain reticence eventually gave way to firm opposition. That reaction in turn led to his condemnation by the authorities charged with maintaining public order. He died by crucifixion at Jerusalem. At that time, this was the political capital and holy city of the Jewish people. He was born into that people about thirty years earlier.

However, the story does not end with his death. Some of those who had heard and followed him claimed to have seen him alive again after his death, and this news spread across time and place. Thus, there came into being what we call "Christianity." Today, the Christian faith counts more than 1.5 billion members, spread throughout the world.

All the questions raised here come down to one: How could all this happen? What exactly can we know about Jesus? What can possibly cast light on how he deserved such a destiny, such an impact, and such a "survival"? Yes, how can we explain all that; and just as importantly, what does all this teach us about ourselves?

We need to acknowledge something right from the start: such an "explanation" presupposes that we can describe the life "this Jesus" lived and that we can convey the message he communicated by his teaching and activity. We must also be able to clarify his identity and even explain the movement he began that continues in our own time. History, message, identity, posterity: these are the major headings of the questions we will treat in our plan to "explain Jesus to everyone."

The first objective will be to clarify what we can really know about this individual. Virtually everyone has heard of him and knows at least something about his importance among the great figures of humanity. We will apply the methods of historical science and the type of critical reflection that defines that science and puts it to work.

Obviously, we cannot ignore or neglect what believing Christians have understood, said, and proclaimed concerning this same individual across the centuries. Put simply, we will try to identify the reasons they could have in taking their positions about him and in speaking about him as they have. They go so far as to recognize in this man a god, and they see in him the very revelation of "the one God, living and true"! We should be able to reach our precise goal even if it does not compel a response of faith from the one to whom we are explaining.

There is no reason to hide the fact that I am a believing Catholic Christian, a theologian (of the Faculty of Theology and Religious Sciences of the Catholic Institute of Paris for more than twenty-five years) and even a bishop (now retired from the Archdiocese of Strasbourg, where I exercised that office from 1997–2007). Readers may well think that my identity certainly qualifies me to speak about Jesus. At the same time, they may fear that this may make me not just a partisan but also a propagandist, despite all my efforts to the contrary.

I invite you to judge on the evidence. The way I understand my responsibility as a believer, as a theologian, and as a pastor has always forbidden me to yield to any form of proselytism or clericalism, in whatever way these terms can be understood.

While I am confident that I have good reasons to believe what I believe about Jesus, I acknowledge that (1) it is a question of *faith*, and not a self-evident certitude; and (2) it is, therefore, incumbent upon me to present this faith in an intelligible manner (in its essential content, its motivations, and its value) even to people who do not adhere to it and who do not necessarily even consider adhering to it.

It seems to me that a "testimony" proposed in a responsible manner is something entirely different from an attempt to solicit faith in an indirect way. My guide here will be the great French author Charles Péguy. He said, "When I see my friend coming my way [and I personally dare to say that I am entirely disposed to consider every reader a friend], my first thought is not to say to myself: 'How can I brainwash him?'"

1

HISTORY

Did Jesus really exist? Are we dealing with a historical person or with a total myth?

We certainly must raise this question right at the beginning of our study! It would be pointless to talk about a historical figure if we cannot be sure that he even existed. In the nineteenth and twentieth centuries, that existence was called into question, and even to this day doubts are sometimes raised.

In the nineteenth century there appeared the "mythical school." This school of thought held that Jesus was simply the product of human imagination. The philosopher Paul-Louis Couchoud (1879–1959) was the principal representative of this school in France. He was important enough that the philosopher of religion Jean Guitton felt obliged to discuss Couchoud's positions in his works about Jesus and the origins of Christianity. In Germany, the liberal Protestant theologian David Friedrich Strauss (1808–74) and the Tübingen school of F. C. Baur put forward the same position.

The proponents of the mythical school affirmed that the figure of a god appearing in human form to help his followers before returning to his heavenly dwelling appears regularly in the history of religions. This, they argue, must cast doubt on what Christians say about Jesus. These thinkers also point out that at the winter solstice (the precise moment of the year when daylight begins to drive back the darkness of the long nights), the ancient Romans celebrated the feast of the *Sol invictus*. This marked the victory of the sun god over darkness and death. In the fourth century, Christians chose that moment for the Feast of Christmas, the birth of Jesus. They simply substituted their Christian feast for a feast of the dominant pagan religion. For members of this school this fact explains why Christians presented their Jesus as "the dawn from on high [who] will break upon us, to give light to those who sit in darkness and in the shadow of death, to guide our feet into the way of peace" (Luke 1:78–79), and eventually as "the true light, which enlightens everyone" (John 1:9), and "the light of the world" (John 9:5). Furthermore, as the resurrection of Jesus was often associated with the rising of the phoenix from its own ashes, these thinkers insisted that his story belongs in the category of legend rather than history.

We could expand the list of arguments offered by this mythical school. All its proponents rejected the historical existence of Jesus. For them, everything regarding his personality, behavior, and destiny belongs to the category of "myth." They went on to say that the "concocted testimonials" concerning a so-called Jesus were simply inventions, or frankly deceptions. They concluded that the original fable made sense to gullible people who were easily impressed by awesome events and impressive characters. They in turn passed on the story without question.

However, the situation soon changed. As the mythical school was developing, a critical historical scientific method was also providing another way of investigating historical events and persons. This new method immediately set out to examine the evidence for the existence of "a certain Jesus" in a time, a place, and context identified with enough precision that doubting the existence of Jesus in human history was no longer possible.

Once his historical existence has been established, is this Jesus the same as the one we call Jesus Christ?

Yes, indeed! But before continuing our study, we must make an important distinction in our research and reflection on the individual we are considering. In the title of this work and throughout its first chapter, we have stayed with the designation Jesus. But everyone knows that he is also frequently called Jesus Christ. We need to pay attention to this difference. If the two terms identify the same person, each term approaches and designates him from a different point of view. The first term—*Jesus*—refers directly to the actual human reality and destiny of a man among men, called *Yeshou/Jeoshua/Joshua/* Jesus. The second term—*Christ*—always refers to this same concrete human existence of Jesus. However, it designates and acknowledges him (or, "confesses him in faith") as the Messiah and therefore *Christos*/Christ. *Christos*/Christ says in Greek what *Mashiah*/Messiah says in Hebrew. In short, the one who appeared to all his contemporaries as Jesus was identified and professed by his followers as Christ/Messiah. Therefore, these followers came to be called *Christianoi*/Christians. We must consider what all this presupposes, signifies, and implies.

In the first part of this book we will examine all that concerns Jesus from a historical point of view and what we can say about his human life. Only afterward can we focus on what it means to complete "this Jesus" with the designation "the Christ."

How can we be sure that Jesus existed? What are the undeniable proofs?

JESUS EXPLAINED

When examining any event, figure, or period, a historian can only work on the basis of *sources*. The principal ones are texts. Archeological remains are also valuable in dealing with ancient history. Eyewitnesses can prove decisive when dealing with current events. In the case of Jesus, who lived twenty centuries ago, archeological discoveries are very interesting. However, for the most part, we must depend on written sources that are still available to us today.

So, we begin with the archeological evidence. Discoveries during the last century have taught us a great deal about Jerusalem in the time of Jesus. It is worth noting that the praetorium where he was condemned to death and the path he trod through the main streets of the city to the site of his crucifixion have been identified, thanks to excavations systematically carried out by specialists. But even more important is the discovery of an inscription in the theater of Caesarea, to the south of Mount Carmel. It mentions Pilate who presided at the trial of Jesus. It also provides his precise title of "Prefect."

Is that all we have to establish the existence of Jesus with certainty?

It is by no means insignificant, for it clearly establishes a link with the Gospels, which are by far the principal texts recording the life of Jesus. Before turning to them, it is worthwhile to cite some other texts. These are even more compelling because they were written by non-Christian writers. These authors certainly had no interest in trying to convince people of the existence of Jesus. There are not many of these, but they are clear and unambiguous.

The historian Suetonius (ca. 70–128, cited in *The Life of Claudius*, 25, 4) reports that in the year 49 (or perhaps as early as 41) of our era, the emperor "banished from Rome all the Jews, [at least that part of them who called themselves Christians], who were continually making disturbances at the instigation of one *Chrestus*." In a letter to Trajan (*Letters*, 10, 96), Pliny the Younger (ca. 61–62, v. 114) informs the emperor about those people who offer worship "to Christ, as to a god." Even more explicit is the testimony of the Jew Flavius Josephus (after 100, *The Antiquities of the Jews*, XVIII, 63–64), who makes a clear distinction between "Jesus" and "Christ." He writes,

> Now there was about this time Jesus, a wise man; he was a doer of wonderful works, a teacher of such men as received the truth with pleasure. He drew over to him both many of the Jews and many of the Greeks....And when Pilate, at the suggestion of the principal men among us [these were the Jewish authorities], condemned him to the cross, those that loved him at the first did not cease doing so.... And the tribe of Christians, [so named because of him,] are not extinct at this day.

There is also the following text from the *Annals* of the Roman Tacitus (ca. 55–119) before the year 120 (Book 15, section 44): "To suppress the rumor [that Nero had ordered the fire that burned Rome in 64], he falsely charged with the guilt, and tortured the group called Christians. Their name comes from Christus, who was put to death by Pontius Pilate, procurator of Judea in the reign of Tiberius."

Are these the only non-Christian texts that speak about Jesus? There are not very many of them.

Nonetheless, there are enough to declare that it is no longer possible to doubt the existence of Jesus. We find him clearly mentioned by witnesses. Some of them are total strangers to his followers, or even hostile to members of his immediate posterity.

Still working outside the Christian community, we can consider texts from ancient Judaism that refer to the "Jesus of history." In addition, there are the Gospels and the other writings called "apocryphal." These documents were not officially adopted by Christians into the "canon"[1] of the New Testament. While this literature teaches us about the Jewish culture of the period between the Old and New Testaments, known as the "intertestamental period" and a little beyond, it does not provide anything substantial or significant about the history and the historicity of Jesus.

The famous manuscripts of the Dead Sea Scrolls were discovered in the eleven grottoes of Qumran beginning in 1947. At the time of Jesus, an Essene community lived there in retreat from the world. These documents are very helpful in clarifying the social and cultural environment in which Jesus lived; but they contain no direct reference to the man of Nazareth.

Gnostic[2] writings were discovered in 1954 at Nag Hammadi, in Egypt. Among these documents *The Gospel of Thomas* (written toward the end of the second century) records 114 "sayings of Jesus." Some of them certainly seem authentic. They teach us about the links of the first Christian groups with the Mediterranean and Asiatic world conquered by Alexander the Great. They also inform us about the influence of that world on Hebrew life and culture in the period, including Palestine.

In the texts of rabbinic Judaism,[3] the Mishna and the two Talmuds, Jesus is occasionally mentioned (some 15 references), but it is in derogatory terms. These represent superficial echoes of a more or less declared polemic between Jews and Christians rather than historic sources providing reliable information about the Jesus of history.

If the existence of Jesus has been established, what do we know with certainty about his life? You have spoken of the Gospels. Are they trustworthy?

As we have just seen, non-Christian witnesses give us certainty concerning the existence of a Jesus of history. However, we must recognize from the outset that they provide very little information about his life and identity. The only sources available to us that cast more light on these questions are documents called the "canonical" Gospels, which constitute a large part of the New Testament.

These writings are far from being a genuine biography of Jesus! They certainly cover the path that leads from his conception and birth to the end of his life. They have a lot to offer about his words and actions along with the reactions of the various groups who heard him speak. But these four Gospels are not in complete agreement with each other on all points. Moreover, they do not give us any information on entire periods in the life of their "hero." Essentially, they bring to our attention actors, authorities, and powers that are far beyond the ordinary experience of human life: God the Father, the Holy Spirit, angels, Satan, demons, and so on. Finally, the historical existence that they present to us only takes on all its consistency and significance in relation to a before and an after located in God: The God from whom "this Jesus" appears to have come and to whom he tells us he has returned. Yet, to tell the truth, he had never actually left the presence of God—since Jesus himself was ultimately recognized as God!

There is one surprising fact: the evangelists who bear witness to Jesus only do so by rereading the events of his life through the eyes of a faith that was born with his resurrection three days after his death! The evangelists make clear that those who followed Jesus frequently misunderstood the events at the time when they took place. Nonetheless, in the Gospels these events were interpreted as the unexpected revelation that "this man" had a bond with God that was entirely unique.

But that means that the Gospels are already an interpretation of the life of Jesus with a view to spreading faith in him. Therefore, can they teach us anything that is historically certain?

The only witnesses who can enlighten us on his historical existence are those who appear in the New Testament, and they take him for "more than simply Jesus." Therefore, there is only one way to approach this question. It is a matter of trying to establish if and to what extent the gospel sources convey elements that (1) enable us to see him as his contemporaries had discovered him and shared his company; and (2) are effectively accessible to us today with enough certainty, thanks to an appropriate method of studying them.

How can we distinguish or recognize these historical elements in the New Testament, if they take Jesus for more than a man?

Here, we must begin by describing the methods used in exegesis of the New Testament documents. In other words, how can we draw out their true meaning? The word *exegesis* comes from a Greek verb meaning to "bring forth." So, the goal of a scientific way of reading the Bible is to "draw out or extract" from the text the meaning(s) that it conveys. Scholars did not always have the means to treat biblical texts historically, because the scientific method for doing so was not yet invented. Even when it came into being, it was not always applied to this kind of text. So, there was practically no distinction between a scientific approach and a doctrinal approach (which could be very refined). Basically, scholars thought that the New Testament "told the truth" about Jesus. They did not know how to distinguish between the Jesus of history and the Christ of faith, between the historical aspect (his concrete existence: the here and now of the person presented in the Gospels: Jesus) and a doctrinal–theological dimension (his resurrection and especially his divinity: the Christ).

Obviously, people could accept or reject the New Testament, along with the Church that proclaimed it. They could be interested in it or not. They could also receive what it had to say about Jesus selectively, that is, to the extent that they personally found it plausible. But if they really accepted these writings as the Church presented them, they did not have the means to make a distinction between historical facts and the doctrinal ideas contained in them. Consequently, it meant that people either committed themselves to the whole story or rejected all of it. In other words, there was no question of accepting one or another of the sayings or deeds attributed to Jesus and leaving aside the virginal conception or his destiny in the passion and resurrection. In some ways it was a matter of "take it or leave it!"

When did they start to read the New Testament differently? When did they begin to distinguish doctrine from the facts and events reported by the text?

Things began to change in the course of the nineteenth century, when biblical scholars started using scientific and critical methods developed by what was emerging as the science of history. The first step is "establishing" the texts, that is, restoring the stories to their original state by careful study of the documents that transmit them to us. Next comes methodical treatment: studying the larger context of the Near East at the time by means of archeological research and the like. The researchers' goal was to "return to Jesus," the person behind all the "additions" made to him by virtue of belief and doctrine. This was the project that a large German movement took as its task. It was known as the *Leben-Jesu-Forschung* ("historical research on the life of Jesus").

Far from finding the sure, pure, and solid Jesus these scholars hoped to reveal, this approach ended up presenting a wide variety of profiles for Jesus as a political agitator and illusionist or a wonder-worker and spiritual reformer. Even more surprising, Albert Schweitzer (1875–1965), who was an organist and physician as well as a good scripture scholar and theologian, demonstrated that the researchers inevitably wound up presenting Jesus in the light of their own concepts of society and human existence. Ultimately those who read their works learned more about the scholars than they did about Jesus. So much for the first stage of specialized historical research about Jesus.

Then Rudolf Bultmann arrived on the scene (1884–1976). He was a German Lutheran scripture scholar as well as a philosopher and theologian. He started from the premise that it was impossible to depict a historical Jesus who stands apart from any interpretation. In fact, scholars could never arrive at Jesus himself. Instead they could only arrive at what had been said about him in "literary forms" that revealed the living conditions and the situation of believers in the first century who spoke about and then wrote about Jesus. Bultmann continued: We must accept that we cannot really know anything (or almost anything) about Jesus. In fact, he goes on to say that we should not even want to know anything about him. The real question about Jesus is not how to arrive at an objective knowledge about him. Rather—and here it is still Bultmann speaking—we must decide how to engage existentially with the word and follow in the footsteps of this remarkable prophet in order to achieve genuine human "authenticity."

A new upheaval arose in the next generation with Ernst Käsemann (1906–98). This theologian was undoubtedly the most brilliant of Bultmann's disciples. Regardless of what his master at the University of Marbourg may have taught, Käsemann insisted that we can develop a philosophy of knowledge and a method capable of providing trustworthy access to the historical reality of Jesus. Käsemann proposed a certain number of criteria effectively permitting a well-grounded historical discernment. Sparked by the upheaval initiated by Bultmann, the works multiplied around Käsemann and mobilized a multitude of scholars, especially in Germany: J. Jeremias, E. Fuchs, H. Conzelmann, H. Schürmann, G. Bornkamm, and others. This list is not exhaustive, but it is indeed impressive. It marks the beginning of what generally became a second stage of specialized research about Jesus.

In several places, and especially in the United States, these criteria eventually won support from most specialized research scholars. The "third quest" of the historical Jesus includes the Jesus Seminar, primarily under Jewish and Protestant direction, and the masterful research of the Catholic John Meier, *A Marginal Jew*.[4]

You are talking about very learned discussions, are you not?

We will not delve into the details of the research in the last thirty years. Much has been done and the positions vary considerably. For our purposes, it will be most helpful and enlightening to clarify the state of the texts we are working with and examine several general principles of interpretation—especially the valuable criteria we have just mentioned. There is general agreement on applying them.

We begin with some information about the written sources: the "manuscripts of the New Testament." The original copies have disappeared. However, several of the world's great libraries have many ancient papyri and parchments. There are, for example, eighty-eight fragments of papyrus (several dating from the middle of the second century!) and roughly three thousand Greek manuscripts written in capital letters or in cursive script. If we add the Syriac, Coptic, Armenian, and Latin fragments, the liturgical lectionaries, and the citations scattered in the writings of the first centuries, the harvest of the New Testament manuscripts is much more abundant than what we have of any of the authors of classical antiquity, including the Greek Plato and the Roman Cicero. Of course, there are many "variants" among these different manuscripts. Nonetheless, we now have trustworthy editions, which present an original text reconstructed in a critical manner. That text also indicates in footnotes the major differences among the various textual witnesses, carefully studied by specialists.[5]

This new generation of scholars worked at establishing the original texts of the Gospels and other New Testament writings through "critical study of the sources," the various manuscripts available to us. That is, they attempted, as much as possible, to restore the stories to their original state. They were also concerned with dating these different manuscripts and studying how they relate to one another. Of the three Gospels called "Synoptic," because it is possible to lay them out in three parallel columns in order to "see and compare them together," the oldest is the Gospel of Mark (about AD 65). The other two, Matthew and Luke (about AD 80–85) draw from him as well as from what is called the "Q source" (from the German word *Quelle* meaning "source"). This source is undoubtedly a little more ancient, composed in the forties of the first century. The Fourth Gospel, attributed to John, seems to have taken its present form about the year 95. But we must not lose sight of the fact that, before the Gospels were composed, several letters were written by Saint Paul. They also constitute an important part of the New Testament, and they have something to say about Jesus. This is clear in the First Letter to the Thessalonians, which was most certainly written in 50 or 51—barely twenty years after the death of Jesus.

In connection with establishing and dating of the texts, we can then attempt to determine their historical contribution according to various criteria. It is precisely here that the principles or criteria elaborated in Käsemann's famous "NO" to Bultmann come into play.

So, what are these famous criteria that allow us to discern the historical content of the texts?

I will mention just three of them. The first criterion can perhaps be called "multiple attestation." When several independent witnesses (*Q*, Mark, Paul, John, and more) all mention the same words or actions of Jesus, this strongly supports their authenticity.

Then comes a criterion of "difference." Sometimes a gospel passage attributes to Jesus a saying or a deed that does not correspond to what we know about his Jewish environment or the Christian communities that emerged after his death. In such a case it is most reasonable to attribute those words or deeds directly to Jesus. A single but clear example: We are told that Jesus was baptized by John the Baptist. This information must be true. We know that serious tensions existed in the first century between the disciples of the Baptist and the disciples of Jesus. Why then would the disciples of Jesus invent an allegiance of their master to someone they saw as his rival?

A third criterion is "coherence." It is reasonable to maintain as at least plausible words and deeds that are compatible with the results of the first two criteria.

Once conclusions are drawn from these three criteria, it is simply a matter of relating them to one another. Thanks to such a methodology we can get a rather precise and trustworthy representation of the Jesus of history beyond the fact of his historical existence. We have already concluded that his existence is indisputable.

Starting with that, is it possible to propose a sort of "lowest common denominator" regarding the Jesus of history? To begin, what can we say about the way his life unfolded?

There is general agreement among scholars that he was born during the reign of Emperor Augustus, between the year 6 and 4 BC (i.e., at least four years before the date he is usually presumed to have been born). At any rate, it was before the death of Herod the Great, who died in the year 4 BC. As for the place of his birth, some historians favor Nazareth. During his lifetime this locality remained the place of reference for him (after all, he is regularly called "Jesus of Nazareth"). Matthew identifies Bethlehem as the place of his birth. It was the city of King David and it also has a historical (and not only a theological) plausibility.

For all his contemporaries Jesus was known to be the son of Mary, wife of a certain Joseph (Matt 1:18–19). His mother tongue was the Galilean dialect form of Aramaic. He also knew Hebrew, the cultic language of the temple of Jerusalem and of the country's synagogues. He clearly attended these houses of worship on a regular basis. We are told about the one in Nazareth reported in Luke 4:16. He probably also knew Greek.

Around the year AD 27 or 28, he left his family and his hometown of Nazareth. Up until that time he lived in a rural working-class community, and he went to be baptized by John in the Jordan river. This ritual immersion in the water suggests dying, from which one rose purified and living, a symbolic passage to new life. Then Jesus dwelt for a time in the desert, like the Baptist. However, he soon began to work as an itinerant preacher, especially throughout Galilee and around the town of Capernaum and Lake Tiberius (also known as the Sea of Galilee). There he spent his time announcing the coming of the "kingdom of God," insisting on the urgent need of "conversion," and healing the sick by words and deeds. These actions were quickly perceived by those around him as miraculous.

This activity increasingly attracted attention. On the one hand, a group of disciples gathered around him, from which there emerged a subgroup that was eventually designated as "the apostles" ("the Twelve" in the gospel account). On the other hand, his activity and his relative success brought down on him increasing hostility on the part of several socioreligious groups that found him more and more disturbing. This was especially evident from the moment when he decided "to go to Jerusalem," probably in the spring of the year 30 (Luke 9:51).

His critique of the cult practiced at the temple and his "confrontational" behavior upset the priestly aristocracy of the place. A joint agreement of the authorities of the Jewish nation (Jerusalem was under the authority of the high priest Caiaphas) and representatives of the Roman occupying power led to the decision to get rid of him after a botched trial. Pontius Pilate, the Roman Prefect mentioned earlier, condemned him to death by crucifixion.

In the end, Jesus was nailed to a cross outside the gates of the city at a place called Golgotha. At that moment he was abandoned by almost all those who were his closest companions. He had gathered them two days earlier for a "farewell dinner" known as "the Last Supper." Astronomical calculations based on chronological indications in the Fourth (John's) Gospel allow us to estimate that he died on April 7 of the year 30 (Friday the fourteenth of Nisan in the Jewish calendar).

When the Christian tradition speaks of a resurrection of Jesus, is that a myth, an unproven event?

Like the different episodes of the life of Jesus that we have cited as proven facts, it is also verifiable that already in the period between the years 35 and 40, it was reported that his close disciples had started a "rumor" in the days immediately following his burial, that Jesus had been seen alive again! In addition, it is also a proven fact that based on this testimony transmitted orally at first and then put into writing (by snippets in the beginning), the first Christian communities quickly appeared. This happened in Palestine at first, then soon, and progressively, in cities along the Mediterranean coast, thanks especially to the ministry of Paul, as we will see later.

Among other undeniable facts, we know that already in the year 50–51, Paul wrote a letter to the Christians in the Greek city of Thessalonica. Chronologically, this First Letter to the Thessalonians is the earliest document of the New Testament. There we learn that already at that time Jesus was identified as "Christ-Messiah," the "Son of God," and "the Lord" precisely on the basis of belief in his resurrection. This represents a formal affirmation of what came to be the Christian faith in the one known as Jesus Christ. While this statement of faith will need to be refined, it is already a very clear confession of faith claiming to recognize in the Jesus of history the Christ-Messiah of God.

With all that as background, can we still say that Jesus was Jewish?

Without the slightest hesitation the answer is yes! The question we must ask is what "kind" of Jew Jesus could have been. Palestine was sociologically polarized at the time, and we need to know the socioreligious group to which he might have belonged.

The public behavior of Jesus eventually gave him a personal profile different from all the categories in which people have tried to place him. In the end, he cuts a figure that is entirely unique in human history. He consistently defines his personal trajectory exclusively in reference to the environment, the social connections, and ultimately the human situation in which he was born, lived, and was raised during the first thirty years of his life. How could we possibly understand him outside of this setting?

Flavius Josephus throws light onto the different religious groups or movements of that time. First, we might mention the Pharisees (from a word that means "separated"). They distinguished themselves by their resolve to scrupulously observe all the prescriptions of the Law of Moses.[6]

Close to this group is the community of the Essenes (or the "saints"), who added to that description a concern in their order for ritual purity. They gathered in a community of the just and pure who withdrew from the cities because they wanted to live as strangers to any form of compromise with the spirit "of the age." As for the Sadducees, these were important figures very close to the temple of Jerusalem and its priestly class; they were conservative in every respect.

Among other groups, we also must mention the Zealots and the assassins, characterized by their political and military desire to see (and bring about) the end of the Roman occupation. There was also a sect known as the *therapeutae*, marked more by spiritual and strong ascetical demands.

Did Jesus belong to one of these movements?

Among these groups, Jesus clearly appears closer to the scribes, who were specialists of administrative documents, and even to the rabbis of Pharisaic persuasion rather than to the important priestly notables of the Sadducees or the Essene purists. Moreover, we have already said that at least at the beginning of his public life he drew close to the Baptist movement when a certain John the Baptist was gathering followers on the shores of the River Jordan. This John called people to conversion sealed in a baptism that took place by a symbolic plunging in the waters of the Jordan. This ritual marked the decision to change one's life and be reborn in order to prepare for the imminent coming of the "last days."[7] At any rate, we see that immediately after his baptism by John, Jesus made a "retreat in the desert." Then he set out directly on a preaching ministry. This places him very clearly in the general line of the Baptist movement. In many respects this resembles the Pharisaic concern for careful observance of the Mosaic Law.

Were there other preachers like Jesus in Palestine at that time?

With the information we have on the culture and customs of the time when Jesus lived, we are certainly justified in emphasizing this "Nazarene's" role as a preacher (or a rabbi in the large sense of the term). This description fits him better than social agitator or religious reformer, although people have sometimes been inclined to describe him with these terms. Nevertheless, the spiritual inspiration of his message could also have implications for sociopolitical activity or religious and cultural practices.

First, we must note a very distinctive fact about the religious situation of Palestine in the first century of our era: the period was rich in preachers. As Flavius Josephus says in his *Against Apion* (8, 37–42), it was the prevalent opinion among the scribes that the era of prophecy in Israel ended definitively with the disappearance of Zechariah and Malachi, the last prophets of our Old Testament. "The heavens were closed from that time onward." The scribes could only have recourse to what was reported in the ancient texts of the Torah and the oracles of the prophets that had been committed to writing. They studied these documents continually and commented upon them extensively. In other words, the era of the living word had yielded to that of commentaries, debates, and disputes.

Remember that in Israel the prophet is one who, from an etymological point of view "speaks in the place and in the name of God."

Now here comes John the Baptist along with many other "prophets" around him who were speaking once again in the name of God! According to the faith of Israel, this renewal of the divine word signified the "reopening of the heavens." This expression proposed the idea that God had decided to reestablish communication between himself and the world. That, in turn, implied the arrival of the "last days," and thus the "final" or "apocalyptic revelation" (the Greek word *apokalypsis* means "revelation").

The fact that Jesus went to be baptized by John, who was clearly part of this general movement, manifests his intention to place his own ministry in the same framework, along with many others who were engaged in preaching and prophecy. That required him to situate himself in relation to them—that is, to distinguish himself from the others! Now this is what appears shortly afterward: the gospel account clearly states that Jesus denounced "false prophets" (and even "false messiahs") around him.

How and in what way could the respect Jesus had for John the Baptist express a desire to distinguish himself?

Let us be clear: the baptismal act proposed by John and the process of conversion he called for meant that mere fidelity to tradition and simple observance of the prescriptions of the Law were not enough. By going to receive baptism at the hands of John, Jesus took his distance from the ministry of the other preachers who were simply rehashing the oracles of earlier prophets and endlessly repeating appeals to observe the Law's demands. The first message of Jesus was more like that of John the Baptist.

But Jesus would eventually take his distance from John himself. After his brief time in the desert, the man of Nazareth separated completely from the Baptist's circle and established his own group of disciples. For the rest, it is not clear that Jesus ever baptized people himself. If he had done so earlier, he no longer did. In the end, his message is very different from John's. From that time onward, John was seen as the person who came along as a preacher announcing the arrival of the last times, like so many others at the time.

Still considering the historical point of view, what can we know concerning the fact itself and the circumstances of the death of Jesus?

Over the centuries some have denied that Jesus died by crucifixion. The holy book of the Muslims, the Qur'an, for example, shows great esteem for Jesus (whom they call "Issa"). However, it asserts that Jesus was not crucified. But we know that Jesus died because he lived, and he was known by his contemporaries to be a man among other men. Tacitus and Josephus bear witness to his death and even to the fact that he was executed.

This raises two questions: Why and how did Jesus die?

The first question concerns the thorny, conflicted, and persistent problem: who was responsible for the death of Jesus? We know that his death was often and for a long time blamed on the Jewish people. This went so far that until recently they were generally designated as a "deicide people" ("God killers") even in the Catholic liturgy of Good Friday.

We must formally deny that idea for at least three reasons. First, the events in question cannot possibly be the responsibility of an entire people. Even more importantly, twenty centuries separate us from that time! Only the high priests could have been implicated in that affair. The scribes mentioned by the gospel account play a very small role in the story. The cries of the populace are the excessive reaction of an excited crowd and not the reasoned expression of a responsible position taken. A second consideration: we cannot overlook the fact that everything in the opinions and attitudes concerning Jesus was done by Jewish people because the evidence clearly tells us that the followers of Jesus were also Jewish. Finally, and most importantly, we must recognize that Jesus bears responsibility for his own condemnation. We will come back to this point later.[8] His own behavior regarding the Judaism of his times and especially at the temple, together with the perceived risk of social or sociopolitical troubles, provoked the antagonistic reactions leading to his execution.

As for the high priests and the Sanhedrin (the high court of the Jews, of which the high priest was a member), it cannot be said that there was no Jewish implication at all. But that did not take the form of a trial, contrary to the longtime received opinion. Rather, it took the form of a denunciation to the representatives of the Roman power, who alone held responsibility from that moment on for the process of his condemnation.

The denunciation to the political authorities by the leaders of the Jewish nation was clever from two points of view. On the one hand, they had no desire to denounce the juridical powerlessness they lived under during the Roman occupation by conducting a legal procedure leading to an execution. On the other hand, it casts light on the social and political problems that incited Jesus to act and to take the positions that he did. In short, from a formal point of view, the whole process (the arrest, the trial, and the condemnation to death) was entirely the work of the occupying Roman authorities.

Are we sure that Jesus died on a cross? What a terrible form of torture!

Passing from the question of why, we arrive at the question of how. Because his condemnation was Roman, his execution was also Roman. The traditional Jewish method of execution was by stoning. In this case the choice was made for the Roman method of crucifixion. This torture was indeed terrible and especially infamous. After a period of horrible suffering, the victim died from asphyxiation. In principle it was reserved for those guilty of high treason against the state, but at that time it was generally applied to all sorts of "offenders."

The condemned man himself carried the *patibulum*, the wooden beam, which was then fixed to a pole planted in the earth. At its two ends they nailed the forearms of the victim and hoisted his body up in such a way that, according to the received expression, he was "hanged on the gibbet," and exposed to the sight and the jeers of the crowd.

Before that, the condemned man was paraded through the city, carrying the instrument of his torture. He was a living illustration of what people could expect if by their words or behavior they stirred up trouble or were even suspected of doing so. There were many such executions at the time.

Recent archeological excavations have furnished reliable elements concerning the place of judgment where Pilate, the prefect, presided. This work has also identified the itinerary followed by Jesus through the city (the "way of the cross") as well as the place of the execution (Golgotha, from an Aramaic word meaning "skull"; this refers to the form of the rock outside the city where the crucifixion took place). Two "bandits" (Mark 15:27) were crucified with Jesus, one on each side of him. (Their arms were tied to the *patibulum*; the forearms of Jesus were nailed to his cross.) Recent archeological excavations have discovered the body of a man crucified in the first century. This has shown us that the feet of these victims were attached with a single nail passing through their two calcaneus bones. These bones form the projection of the heels, one on top of the other.

Aside from a few individuals standing nearby—John the Apostle and some women accompanying his mother—Jesus died abandoned by his disciples. According to Roman usage, a lance was thrust into his side, piercing his heart, "and at once blood and water came out" (John 19:33–34). The soldiers did not use the usual practice of breaking his legs to speed his death. Afterward he was taken down quickly from his cross. They wanted to finish the process before the imminent celebration of the Passover, the most important feast in the Jewish religion.[9] The evangelist Mark tells us, and it appears well established, that the body of Jesus was then placed in a new tomb. It belonged to a prominent figure who was both sympathetic and generous. His name was Joseph of Arimathea (Mark 15:43–46).

Once the stone was rolled to close the tomb, which had recently been hewn out of rock, his contemporaries no doubt thought that the story of "just one more Nazarene among many others" was concluded. François Mauriac, the great French literary figure and winner of the Nobel Prize for Literature in 1952, observes that, at least on the physical level, the fate of Jesus does not seem very different from that of his fellows. Apparently, Judas gave a sign that allowed the soldiers who had come to seize Jesus in the Garden of Gethsemane to identify him. The traitor told them how they would recognize Jesus in the shadows of the Garden of Olives: "The one I will kiss is the man" (Matt 26:48).

2

MESSAGE

If Jesus was an itinerant preacher among many others in Palestine, can we say that he left his mark on his time and on posterity because he was a wise man, a wisdom master, a sort of Christian Dalai Lama?

The Dalai Lama who travels around the world is an admirable human figure, and his teaching speaks to many of our contemporaries. But I find it a little surprising to bring up this great spiritual leader at this point in our study. For one thing, twenty centuries have already passed between "the man of Nazareth" and the present head of the Tibetans. Surely, many things have changed in the meantime! Then again, the activity of Jesus never took place in the political sphere. He had no need to disengage from it, whereas this high Asian religious figure has felt the need to be politically involved in recent decades. Finally, why would we compare Jesus, who has so profoundly marked the history of our Western world up to the present time, with a person who was relatively unknown in our culture just a quarter of a century ago? We can recognize the truth of this fact whether we believe in Jesus or not.

Nonetheless, are we not dealing in both cases with wise men and even wisdom masters?

The *Jesus Seminar*, a recent trend in American research mentioned earlier has upheld adamantly that "Jesus was entirely a wise man." Those scholars also argue that several characteristics keeping us from reducing him entirely to that category in the past were woven into the gospel's fabric by his disciples later. Drawing especially on the apocryphal Gospel of Thomas, which we have already cited, J. D. Crossan, a leader in the Jesus Seminar, says that Jesus was "a Galilean peasant" who worked as a preacher. However, for Crossan, his message ultimately differs very little from the philosophical school of the Greek cynics (Antisthenes, Diogenes, and the like), which arose four centuries earlier. Crossan believes that a certain number of the "sayings" attributed to Jesus prove his thesis. He cites the following: "Give therefore to the emperor the things that are the emperor's, and to God the things that are God's" (Matt 22:21; see also Mark 12:17; Luke 20:25) and "What does it profit them if they gain the whole world, but lose or forfeit themselves?" (Luke 9:25). The basic idea for Jesus and for the cynics is that inherited customs, conventions, and ideas have no real value in themselves. Therefore, we must renounce the pursuit of riches, power, honors, and even health. All that truly matters is the quest for the one thing necessary. That one thing is the pursuit of wise virtue.

We certainly cannot deny that many of the sayings of Jesus represent a rare and extraordinary human wisdom. On the one hand, this preacher frequently calls people to care for others, to be compassionate, even to be totally available to them. He also invites his hearers to cultivate personal serenity and to put aside worries, great and small alike. In addition, he asks people to be concerned about the one thing necessary[1] (Luke 10:42), without neglecting daily realities. He tells us to concentrate on the here and now, but not to lose sight of the uncertainty that weighs on tomorrow, nor overlook the serious threat that can suddenly wipe out the present (Luke 12:20). He teaches that the tradition of the ancients should be respected, and the prescriptions of the Law be honored. However, he also insists on proper motivation and free decision. Sometimes these values overrule literal observance of the Commandments. He explicitly challenges purely exterior conformity to the behavior prescribed in the Law of Moses.

The gospel writings are filled with brief instructions or simple examples presented by Jesus. We find the same spiritual tone in several more developed passages and gospel discourses. Some of these may represent later elaborations within the communities dedicated to keeping alive the memory of their master. Sometimes they are the result of editing by the final redactors, organizing his sayings in such a way as to draw out all their meaning and implications.

We can conclude this point by underlining two more characteristic traits. First, everything that Jesus teaches about human wisdom comes back to the idea that every human being is in the hands of a *Providential* God, regardless of that person's status or condition. This God takes care of everyone, and in the end, we are asked to entrust ourselves fearlessly to him. This is supreme wisdom. Second, this wisdom is offered not only to the intellectual elite or power elite. It is addressed to everyone, the little as well as the great of this world. We can even say that his teaching gives preference not to the "wise and powerful," but to "the poor and the little ones." His wisdom offers the same radical challenge with which he confronts the often facile and sometimes dubious "worldly wisdom." This latter type of wisdom always gives precedence to the pursuit of success, even when it comes at the cost of dominating or crushing others, and dismissing any sense of service, commitment, generosity, and availability.

How did Jesus teach this wisdom?

Jesus frequently made use of the literary genre of the *parable,* which clearly shows his desire to address the large and general public. Often used in the rabbinic literature of the first century, the parable is first a teaching procedure using one or more comparisons intended to convey a subtle or more demanding message. One example would be the parable of the lost and found sheep: "What do you think? If a shepherd has a hundred sheep, and one of them has gone astray, does he not leave the ninety-nine on the mountains and go in search of the one that went astray? And if he finds it, truly I tell you, he rejoices over it more than over the ninety-nine that never went astray. So, it is not the will of your Father in heaven that one of these little ones should be lost" (Matt 18:12–14).

In dealing with allegory, the details of the story convey the meaning, while the parable speaks by the whole story it employs. It is true that several gospel parables are allegorizing, especially in John's Gospel. Among the allegorizing parables in the Synoptic Gospels we can cite the sower of the seed (Mark 4:13–20), the Good Samaritan (Luke 10:25–37), and the banquet (Matt 22:1–14). In John's Gospel there are the parable of the shepherd and the gate of the sheepfold (John 10:1–18) and the image of the vine (John 15:1–11).

Looking a little more closely, we can quickly perceive that the preference of Jesus for the genre of parables shows that his message

≈ is addressed to the largest number of people because it connects with daily human-life experiences;

≈ is therefore far from announcing great catastrophes and extravagant revelations;

≈ is presented in modest terms; therefore, it can encounter indifference, or even provoke derision;

≈ bears a powerful dynamic capable of working wonders in every human heart and on a grand worldwide scale, like the mustard seed "that someone took and sowed

> in his field; it is the smallest of all the seeds, but when it has grown it is the greatest of shrubs and becomes a tree, so that the birds of the air come and make nests in its branches" (Matt 13:31–32).

But what exactly did Jesus teach? Did he have a message to convey?

There is no way to present the sayings and positions taken by Jesus as if we were dealing with formal courses or doctoral lessons. Let us simply clarify the essential content and the major points of emphasis in what we can call his message.

Fortunately, scholars no longer subscribe to a dichotomy between a Judaism perceived as "legalistic, rigid, tortured, deicide" (this phrase comes from the Swiss biblical scholar Daniel Marguerat) and a Jesus portrayed as the slayer of trivial obsessions and narrow-minded quibbles coming from the Pharisees. In that case, Jesus was presented as the champion of a religion of the heart in opposition to the Law, and of the spirit against the letter.

In fact, research into the Judaism of the period has shown that among the Pharisees there were debates and ways of thinking that were much more open than scholars had assumed for a very long time. Furthermore, recent studies have shown that Jesus shared many of the convictions and practices of his Jewish environment. In fact, many of the teachings and instructions attributed to him in the Sermon on the Mount[2] have at least partial parallels in the (later) large compilation of ancient Jewish tradition known as the Talmud. While the gospel texts available to us set Jesus apart in some ways, they also include his own words, declaring that he did not come "to abolish [the law] but to fulfill [it]." He goes on to say, "not one letter, not one stroke of a letter, will pass from the law until all is accomplished" (Matt 5:17–18).

Despite a period of popular success, Jesus was eventually rejected and condemned, as we have already indicated. There was clearly a shift, a disturbing and dangerous one at that, in relation to his surroundings.

On what precise points did Jesus express the difference of his message? What exactly makes his message unique?

The decisive factor is the radical nature and the urgency of his call. What Jesus preaches and announces, the principal and central content of his teaching, is the coming of the "kingdom of God." That is, the imminent intervention of God himself, for the judgment of the world and for the benefit of all his people and each of its members. Jesus says this is not the time for vacillation, for polemics, for endless arguments. Nor is there time for insisting simply on "strict observance" of the commandments of the Law, or for mutual exclusions. The prescriptions of the Torah are addressed to the heart of those who are ready to put them into practice, inviting them to welcome what God alone can give. Now he lets it be known that he is ready to satisfy the longings of those who are wise enough to open their hearts to his arrival.

If in the end the message is about God, and about access to God that is only possible by his grace,[3] we see clearly that the message of Jesus concerns *God* himself. However, it also clearly implies instruction about human life and about the idea that every individual can have concerning his or her own existence.

Can you be more precise about the message of Jesus?

In the end, we can say that everything he preached was directed by two essential principles.

First, there exists a "living and true" God who can be addressed as "Father." This God is at one and the same time the Creator of all that exists and the Providence who watches over all his children, beginning with the neediest among them. The immediate consequence of this is that those who believe in this God are called to love in truth each of those who are their brothers and sisters. In this they imitate him who "makes his sun rise on the evil and on the good" (Matt 5:45), and who goes so far as to nourish the little birds (6:26). The only way to show that we are worthy "children of your Father in heaven" is to love all human beings who are his children (5:45).

The second essential point that underlies the teaching of Jesus is that human life is called to pass through death. For if the living and true God is indeed "the God of Abraham, the God of Isaac, and the God of Jacob," we must understand, like the French philosopher Pascal and so many others before and after him, that we are talking about a "God not of the dead, but of the living" (Mark 12:26–27; Matt 22:32). The immediate consequence of this is the following: not only is the hope of a resurrection from the dead open to human beings, but from this day forward everyone must take that into account in directing his or her life. Therefore, people must convert. They really must orient their lives based on this essential truth, on "the one thing necessary," as we have already pointed out (Luke 10:41–42; cf. Matt 6:30). It is up to us to draw the conclusions.

Love of others on the one hand, *hope* in God on the other: these two fundamental attitudes that the preaching of Jesus calls everyone to adopt pushes us to ask ourselves *by what title* he can give this preaching such precise content and especially with "authority," as Mark (1:22) tells us. At the same time, we need to know what can support and guarantee the confidence we are invited to place in him. In other words, the question of a third fundamental attitude already points to the *faith* we can have in this Jesus whose essential message invites us to love others and to hope in God.

Before approaching the question of faith, can we continue exploring the contents of the message of Jesus? Did he draw a moral teaching out of it? Is it his message that founded the Christian religion?

We have just spoken about the essential "doctrine" of Jesus. Following a simple plan, we can quickly proceed to the morality he drew from it. In fact, we have already begun to sketch it! However, regarding the preacher and sage that he was, our reflection will certainly have to be more nuanced. Concerning what the doctrine of Jesus contains or implies, we need to distinguish between religion, morality, and spirituality. In each of these areas he has some very distinctive points of emphasis that are unique to him.

To the extent that religion calls us to take a position regarding God, and Jesus invites his conversation partners to do so, should we not begin by examining what is involved in his religion?

His religion certainly sends us back to the God of his fathers, that is, the God of Abraham, Isaac, and Jacob, the God of Moses, of the prophets, and of the 150 psalms attributed to David. All of that came to Jesus through the Holy Scriptures of the Old Testament, as they were passed down to his time. He heard them read (and occasionally read them aloud himself) in the synagogue. The cult he rendered to that God was supported by an attitude of prayer and veneration, of devotions, offerings, and even sacrifices, as required by his people's religion. In line with the great prophetic tradition, Jesus maintains that these cultic practices do not substitute for the *interior* obligation of true adoration. Without that all those practices have no meaning.

The Jewish faith held that the temple was the only place in the entire world where God truly resides. It had become a marketplace. It no longer seemed to have much to do with prayer. So, Jesus denounced the practice of this trade and those responsible for it by turning over the stalls of the famous "temple merchants" and the tables of the money changers installed in the place (Mark 11:15). That provoked the decisive hostility of the priestly class. They already had little sympathy for someone they considered an "imposter," since he was neither a priest nor a scribe. Therefore, he did not appear to have an official leg to stand on. Far from making him appear to be a "sacred functionary," his behavior and his teaching in matters of religion expressed his strong conviction as conveyed in the Gospel of John: "True worshipers will worship the Father in spirit and truth" (John 4:23).

Can we move on to the morality of Jesus? It often seems to be summed up in this single teaching: "You shall love your neighbor as yourself." Is that correct?

Passing from religion to morality is easy. According to Jesus, this statement culminates in the radical bond he established between God's cause and that of every human being. Many gospel teachings go in this direction, even if we cannot prove that every one of them goes back to Jesus. "Not everyone who says to me, 'Lord, Lord,' will enter the kingdom of heaven," but those who do on earth "the will of my Father in heaven" (Matt 7:21). Jesus asks, how can you pretend to love God whom "no one has ever seen" (John 1:18; see also 1 John 4:12), if you do not love your own brother who is his child and whom you do see? (see 1 John 4:12). God said through the great prophets of Israel, "It is mercy I want and not sacrifices" (see Matt 9:13). That establishes the evident and close connection with what we have just discovered about the religion of Jesus. And this mercy must be extended first to those who are the most marginalized: the sick and the excluded, those who have been declared "unclean," women (even those considered to be living a "bad life"), and children always!

For all that, Jesus does not neglect the prescriptions of the Jewish Law, the Torah. On the contrary, he frequently mentions a certain number of them. But he is relentlessly preoccupied with denouncing legalism, conformity, and casuistry. When the Pharisee in Matthew's Gospel intends to embarrass Jesus, he pointedly asks him, "Which commandment in the law is the greatest?" (22:36). This is indeed a loaded question. In choosing a single law above all the others he could seem to devalue all the rest. However, Jesus seizes the opportunity of this interrogation to propose a key to understanding *all* morality: in any case, it can only be a way of practicing love: a love that is oriented to both God and neighbor together. For if the first commandment is "You shall love the Lord your God with all your heart, and with all your soul, and with all your mind," the second is "like it" and can never be separated from it: "You shall love your neighbor as yourself" (Matt 22:37–39). In the end the problem is not to know "who is my neighbor" (Luke 10:29). On the contrary, it is to determine to whom I must *make myself* a neighbor (Luke 10:36), among all those to whom God has resolved to make himself a neighbor. There can be no exclusions. More precisely, the "other" can also be the "neighbor" whose ways of acting, inattentiveness, and other undesirable traits could very well make me want to avoid that person and keep my distance.

Why did you previously distinguish a third aspect in the message: namely spirituality? How is that distinct from religion?

In fact, what we call spirituality necessarily accompanies religion and morality. What we have already said has sufficiently cleared the field, so that we may respond in this domain unequivocally. Spirituality, spiritual life, or life "according to the Spirit" (as opposed to life "according to the letter," that is, without personal engagement), does not propel us into *another* life than the one we have here and now. For if there is and if there can be "eternal life," Jesus tells us that it is at work in us already from this day forward. The purity and holiness required of us do not call us to withdraw from this world but to live in the heart of the world in submission to the Spirit of love. That Spirit is capable of "renew[ing] the face of the earth" (Ps 104:30), by first renewing the human heart.

Coming after Jesus, but always faithful to his inspiration, the author of the Fourth Gospel gives us an enlightening formulation: the disciples of Jesus are asked to distinguish carefully between "being in the world" and "being of the world." Being *in* the world is obvious (where else could Christians live?), and it flows directly from their faith in God who "so loved the world that he gave his only Son" (John 3:16). Being *of* the world, on the other hand, implies pursuing immediate success and superficial accomplishments, maximum profit and egotistical self-interest.

It is not tomorrow or the day after that we must set out on the path to this life, for "this very night your life is being demanded of you" (Luke 12:20). The Sermon on the Mount is fundamentally the "charter" of the kingdom of God. The generation after Jesus believed that it summed up his entire vision of spirituality. It is very significant that these values are presented as "Beatitudes" rather than commandments. Note the next to the last of these: "Blessed are the peacemakers, for they will be called children of God" (Matt 5:9). The inaugural statements from the Sermon on the Mount in Matthew 5:1–11 not only invite others to observe certain demands, but more importantly to receive the happiness that can result from putting them into practice.

What do we know about the activity of Jesus? What exactly did he do? How did he behave?

Everything we read suggests that Jesus acted in line with what he boldly taught others to do. In calling others to *trust* in the present, to maintain *hope* for the future, and in all things to give priority to *love*, he could only strive by his own behavior to cast light on these principles and give an example to those who would come to him, remain in his company, and follow him. That certainly seems to have contributed in large part to his success. The author of the New Testament Book The Acts of the Apostles sums up in a few lines the life of Jesus, which had just come to an end, in the following formula: "He went about doing good and healing all who were oppressed by the devil, for God was with him" (Acts 10:38). Obviously, this description is a rather general statement. However, it is quite thought-provoking, for it presents Jesus as someone who was always preoccupied with others and their well-being. He was like a "just man" amid his people! However, beyond the good works he accomplished, which describe the very portrait of a good man, we should also note actions that can be described as "surprising behaviors." We will look at a few of the ones that are among the most historically corroborated.

We might consider first the privileged place he gave to children. In the Palestine of his day, people certainly did not mistreat children. However, they were very far from treating them the way that Jesus did. Occasionally he embraced them. One fine day he placed one of them in the center of a group that had assembled around him and declared, "Truly I tell you, unless you change and become like children, you will never enter the kingdom of heaven. Whoever becomes humble like this child is the greatest in the kingdom of heaven" (Matt 18:3–4; see also Mark 10:13–16). The way Jesus related to women is also extraordinary. The rabbis of the period never allowed women into the group of their followers. Jesus welcomed some of them and included them in the group of disciples that "followed him" (Luke 8:2–3). Still another behavior that was astonishing, and even scandalous for his followers: he chose to dine with "sinners and tax collectors" (Mark 2:16).[4] To these behaviors we must add his cleansing of the temple, which clearly provoked a strong hostile reaction.

Aside from these astonishing behaviors, miracles are also attributed to Jesus. How is that possible if Jesus was really a historical personage?

Here it is important to underline that for Jesus, the attitudes and surprising behaviors we have already mentioned were in no way designed to attract attention. Nor were they a matter of being carried away by strong emotion of the moment. He relates them directly to his message. His words *announce* the coming of the kingdom and call others to change their behavior. His actions show that the kingdom of God is *already* present and active in the world. Now, this will become ever more manifest in connection with the actions that go beyond even his extraordinary conduct, and which today we call "miracles."

We have already mentioned that Flavius Josephus presents Jesus as a "wonder-worker." To confirm that he was indeed perceived in this way, we can offer at least two reasons. At that time there were many other healers, wonder-workers, and exorcists (those who expel demons) in Israel. After all, it was a time when people were preoccupied with the question of salvation, understood primarily as healing and survival. Cults of healing gods flourished at Pergamum, Delphi, and Epidaurus. In addition, general opinion at the time held that a person sent by God authenticated that mission precisely through the signs and wonders he worked. We can therefore affirm that Jesus would not have attracted attention if he had not accomplished at least some of these.

That being said, we will leave aside the signs that are sometimes called "nature miracles," like walking on water (Matt 14:22–33), the multiplication of the loaves (Luke 9:12–17), or the calming of the storm (Mark 4:35–41; Luke 8:22–25). In fact, several exegetes share the opinion that the factual information behind these events is very difficult to determine today. However, the purpose in recounting the events appears to be less a matter of reporting in detail what happened. It is more a matter of rereading them in light of the meaning of the whole life story of Jesus, as seen through the eyes of faith *after* his resurrection from among the dead. Moreover, right at the beginning of the public life of Jesus, the story of the temptations in the desert (Matt 4:1–11) shows that Jesus was determined to avoid any hint of seeking popular success and any ostentatious demonstration of self-promotion or celebrity. Consequently, when he fears that this might happen, he refuses to do a "deed of power" (Mark 6:5); or he makes clear that the proper understanding of his mission requires the rejection of the "spectacular."

All things considered, we can even say that the amount of material recounting the twenty-seven miracles recorded in the Gospels represents a relatively small part of the whole story. Jesus never set about curing all the lepers and paralytics in the Israel of his day. And we never get the impression that he was looking to add more of them to his list, in any sense of the word! He began by calling people to faith and to trust in the moment when he was acting. He always feared ambiguity. Whenever he worked a miracle, he systematically avoided promoting credulity and superstition. He often commanded silence about the miracle. That is certainly a strange way to seek attention!

Two examples: When Jesus agrees to heal a paralytic at Capernaum, he makes it clear that he did not come into this world in order to magically deliver all people from all their bodily suffering. On the contrary, it was to open the way for them to spiritual liberation from sin and evil that held them in subjection (Mark 2:1–5). If he came to the aid of a leper, it was to make clear that when he touched the sick man, he himself was not rendered unclean. Quite the contrary, his touch was healing for the one who was suffering. That is a significant reversal!

> When Jesus had come down from the mountain, great crowds followed him; and there was a leper who came to him and knelt before him, saying, "Lord, if you choose, you can make me clean." He stretched out his hand and touched him, saying, "I do choose. Be made clean!" Immediately his leprosy was cleansed. Then Jesus said to him, "See that you say nothing to anyone; but go, show yourself to the priest, and offer the gift that Moses commanded, as a testimony to them." (Matt 8:1–4)

In short, no matter how you choose to look at things, three points are clear regarding the question at hand. First, Jesus most assuredly exercised the activity of a wonder-worker and exorcist, but he was not the only person to do these things in his time. Second, he set himself apart from the others radically in the sense that in performing his miracles, he wanted nothing to do with using these miraculous events to enhance his glory as a healer or to guarantee the success of his projects.

Third and finally, his surprising actions pose the question of knowing "by whose name" or "by what authority" (Luke 20:2) he could proceed here as he did. Concretely, this means that we must look more closely at his real intentions. Just as importantly, we must ask what qualified him to intervene in such an astonishing way. In other words, it is all about his personal identity. This is suggested by a discussion of his authority, as reported by Matthew: "If it is by the Spirit of God that I cast out demons, then the kingdom of God has come to you" (12:28).

What you have said about the words and actions of Jesus gives us a certain idea of his "way of being human." Can you say more about the kind of man he was, his personality, and even his physical appearance, his "look"?

We will deal with the last point first. We do not know what Jesus looked like: his height and weight, whether he had a beard, or the color of his eyes. Regarding all that, we just must accept the limits of our information.

As to his psychological profile however, it is entirely possible to glean some precise indications providing a reasonably clear picture. To begin, we find that he had the characteristics of true humanity. He was a little child "wrapped in bands of cloth" (Luke 2:12). He had to grow "and became strong, filled with wisdom; and the favor of God was upon him" (Luke 2:40). His mother was named Mary and her husband was Joseph. We are also told that when he was about twelve years old, at the end of a family pilgrimage to Jerusalem, he caused his parents a great deal of anxiety by separating from them for more than a day (Luke 2:41–50).

We know that he was a caring individual and capable of friendship. We can mention here at least Lazarus and his two sisters, Martha and Mary, at Bethany (John 11:1–5), as well as a disciple named John, and another known as Mary Magdalene. He suffered hunger and thirst. He appreciated a good meal and a glass of wine; for that indulgence "the well-intentioned people" (as the French singer and songwriter Georges Brassens identifies them) called him "a glutton and a drunkard" (Luke 7:34). (Here is another example where the criterion of "difference," previously discussed, can clearly be applied!) The gospel account shows his disappointment in the face of the indifference and growing hostility toward him on the part of his contemporaries. This frustration is even stronger when he sees these attitudes aimed at others, especially the disadvantaged, the suffering, the marginalized, and even those who were excluded from society.

But these last elements lead us to a second meaning of the term *human*. Not only do we find in Jesus all the qualities of the "human condition" in all its reality, but he also interacts with other people gracefully and respectfully. The fact that "the good Samaritan" was not a Jew does not exclude this man of mercy from deserving full consideration (Luke 10:33). When a young man heard the call of Jesus and turned away, his departure does not make Jesus care for him less (Matt 19:16–22). The fact that a woman has been leading a questionable life does not mean that she should be rejected (Luke 7:36–50; see also John 8:1–11 with its allusion to stoning). And if a little old lady has put only a small coin into the temple treasury, people should not underestimate her generosity (Luke 21:1–2). We could add many more characteristics, reflections, and behaviors that confirm that Jesus belonged to our human condition. They also show clearly that in all circumstances he made himself the "neighbor" of those he encountered.

He calmly treats every person as an individual with *equal dignity*, and thus worthy of total respect. In short, he treats everyone as a brother or a sister. And the more this dignity, respect, and fraternity mark those in peril, Jesus shows that it is even more important to bear witness of it to them.

We never find the slightest trace of condescendence in him, and still less any contempt. On the contrary, he shows the greatest attention to the "least of these who are members of [his] family," as he will say in presenting the dramatic scene of the "Last Judgment" in Matthew 25:31–46. Jesus is not only "human," but he consistently acts "humanely," as the saying goes!

Jesus is also a strong person, capable of opposing his environment. Does he not clearly set himself apart from it?

Indeed. His behavior in the temple at the age of twelve is already revealing on that point. There he shows a genuine emancipation from his parents, but he also demonstrates his capacity to engage in a serious debate with the dignitaries of that holy place. His relationship with John the Baptist goes in this direction as well. He was capable of assuming his own position in relation to the prophet to whom he presented himself at the beginning of his public life. Soon thereafter he was ready to clarify the difference between them and to establish his own group of followers independent of John's.

Progressively thereafter, Jesus defends himself in words and actions in the face of the resistance, criticism, polemics, and hostilities of the various groups and public figures who found him disturbing. When the time came, he resolutely decided to "go up to Jerusalem," fully aware of the risk he was taking. When he preached in his hometown, the crowd became so "filled with rage" that they wanted to throw him off a nearby cliff. We are told that "he passed through the midst of them and went on his way" (Luke 4:16–30).

He is sometimes ironic, for example during his trial before Pilate and Caiaphas. Far from appearing intimidated by them, he responds with a certain haughtiness. He turns their questions back on them in a way that must have been embarrassing for them. He was also capable of anger, not only against the merchants in the temple, but also toward those who "grieved" him by "their hardness of heart" (Mark 3:5). On the contrary, he was also capable of showing strong sensitivity and real vulnerability. His friendship was a source of sadness and trial. We see him weeping at the tomb of the dead Lazarus (John 11:33–35), and again he weeps over Jerusalem on foreseeing its destruction (Luke 19:41). He himself speaks of his overwhelming fear in the face of the supreme trial that he knows is about to begin. The Letter to the Hebrews communicates a profound truth when it tells us that "Jesus offered up prayers and supplications, with loud cries and tears, to the one who was able to save him from death" (Heb 5:7).

We see it clearly: when we follow the gospel account attentively, there are many specifics that provide a relatively detailed portrait of Jesus. He is far from being "the meek Galilean dreamer" that the French philosopher Ernest Renan saw in him or "the sweet-tempered carpenter with the big soft eyes," an image of Jesus that suggests a certain kind of piety. He is also very different from a political or revolutionary agitator, a savage vigilante, or a haughty and heavy-handed schoolmaster.

But Jesus has often been presented as a revolutionary. Has he not?

The fact that Jesus is sometimes presented as a "political" or even revolutionary figure obliges us to address this question. Jesus makes his position clear in his formal statement: "Give therefore to the emperor the things that are the emperor's, and to God the things that are God's" (Matt 22:21; see also Luke 20:25). Obviously, there were in his entourage, and even among his close disciples, people who wanted him to be the hoped-for "messiah," capable of leading an uprising of the Jewish people against the Romans; this was certainly what the Zealots desired. It is also clear that his teachings and behavior could have led to religious and political disturbances in the public order. We know that this very charge was leveled against him at his trial. But his personal position, revealed by his consistent attitude, is summed up clearly in his declaration to the public powers during that trial: "My kingdom is not from this world" (John 18:36). After his strict refusal to endorse such a title, it was pure mockery when the Romans affixed the inscription "King of the Jews" above his head on the cross; that plaque also identified him as Jesus of Nazareth (John 19:19).

In the end, Jesus appeared as a good and resolute man, determined and sensitive, an educator and a leader, certainly eager to "form" those who followed him. But he was always calling those he was training to freedom. In the end, he could put his life in danger and give it up in the conviction that this was the best way "to make it truly alive."

We would certainly understand Jesus better if we knew more about his education. What do we know about his childhood, his family, and the environment in which he was raised?

We know the names of his parents: Mary and Joseph. The Gospel of Luke tells us that when he was about to be born, his parents had to go to Judea[5] to be counted in the census ordered by the Roman governor. This identifies their geographical heritage. But they lived in Galilee (Matt 2:22–23), a largely rural region. And Jesus most likely spent his first thirty years in this Jewish social environment, living under Roman oppression. He apparently worked as an artisan, following in the footsteps of his father; tradition says he was a woodworker or carpenter (Mark 6:3). We have no way of knowing if he worked on the restoration of the city of Sepphoris, which Herod Antipas was rebuilding near the lake of Tiberias, close to the family home of Jesus.

The New Testament speaks about his brothers and sisters? Did he really have any? This question is even more important since Christian tradition affirms the virginity of his mother Mary!

First, we will look at the question of brothers and sisters. Even among Christians and Catholics, a certain number of New Testament scripture scholars consider that the words "brothers and sisters," used several times in reference to Jesus (e.g., Mark 6:3), must mean what they usually signify! At the same time, we cannot ignore the fact that, from the beginning and throughout the centuries, Christian faith has presented Jesus as the only son of his mother, Mary. Moreover, tradition has indeed affirmed that his mother was a virgin. So, what should we think? Should we think that the word *brothers* could also include cousins at that time? Or could these "brothers and sisters" in question be children of a first marriage of Joseph who was older than his new spouse Mary? Scientific research on the texts may seem to call the "traditional reading" into question. Honestly, however, if Jesus really did have brothers and sisters, why would he have entrusted his mother to the apostle John (John 19:26–27) when he was about to die on the cross?

Regarding the very important but separate question concerning Mary's virginity, I will simply present here one brief theological consideration. If, after his resurrection (and we will have to talk about that subject soon), Jesus experienced a completely unique manner of *leaving* the historical earthly condition, why could his manner of *entering* it not also be "unique"?

Whatever may be the case on that precise point, everyone, believer or not, should recognize an important fact in the gospel accounts. While it may well be surprising, it is evident that Jesus often relativized family ties. When he was just twelve years of age, his parents found him in the temple after three days of searching for him. His mother reproaches their son for causing them so much anxiety by separating from their supervision for more than a day (Luke 2:46). Her complaint seems reasonable to us, but his response shows some resistance. During the wedding feast at Cana, when his mother lets him know there is not enough wine for the feast, he replies in a way that is at least surprising. After asking her how that concerns either of them, he goes on to say, "My hour has not yet come" (John 2:4). One day, his disciples let him know "your mother and your brothers are standing outside, wanting to see you." (Mark tells us that they thought he had lost his mind, see Mark 3:21). He responds brusquely, "My mother and my brothers are those who hear the word of God and do it" (Luke 8:19–21). In a general way, Jesus puts his disciples on guard against overestimating the bonds of flesh and blood in questions of religion, morality, and spirituality: the disciple of the kingdom must be ready to abandon house or field, but also mother and father to follow him, into a "community" of a very different order (see Mark 1:16–20; 3:31–35; Luke 14:26).

Was Mary Magdalene the companion or wife of Jesus? Was he married?

Nothing indicates that Jesus could have been married, even to the famous Mary Magdalene.[6] However, we have reason to think that he had a true and close relationship with her. Celibacy, therefore, is a new characteristic that distinguishes Jesus and John the Baptist from all the priests, rabbis, and other religious figures of the day (except for the Essenes).

Yet we know that he did establish close relationships with several persons such as his friend Lazarus; Mary and Martha, the sisters of Lazarus; as well as the one known as "the beloved disciple." This disciple named John appears to have been the only one to accompany Mary and several other women at the foot of his cross (John 19:25–27).

Did his preaching and, more generally, his public activity attract many disciples?

As soon as Jesus began to speak in public, some of his hearers paid attention to him, followed him, and gathered around him. However, it seems that in a general way we should not exaggerate the designation of "disciples." A variety of motives seem to have been at play here, from pure curiosity or plain sympathy to resolute and constant attachment. Do not be misled by the mention of "crowds" around Jesus, except perhaps in extraordinary circumstances.

Within this vast environment, however, Jesus quickly began to constitute a more limited circle of those who would be charged with his mission and represent him after his departure. Mark (1:16–20) tells us that this was even his first concern and this task of assembling a group would lead to what would soon be called "the Church." We will come back to that theme.

The circle of his closest followers is what the Gospels call the "apostles," or more precisely, "the Twelve." Mark (3:13–19), Matthew (10:1–4), and Luke (6:13–16) all give us a list of their names. This number twelve clearly refers to the twelve tribes of Israel. For the one who announces the coming of the kingdom this choice clearly reveals his direct intention to lay the foundations for a new people of God. From that moment onward, this people will assemble around the apostles and their word, called to the work of passing on the word of their master across time and space.

What type of relationship did Jesus establish with the persons he encountered, those who listened to him, or those he met in passing?

In the accounts given to us by Luke and John, several important personal encounters can give us an idea of the delicacy and the quality of the communication Jesus established. This must have been one of his chief concerns. Remember three occasions: the rich young man (Mark 10:17–22; Luke 18:18–23), the Samaritan woman (John 4:7–29), and finally, the "woman caught in...adultery" (John 8:4–11).

For example, look at Luke's account of the encounter with the "rich young man." He asked Jesus,

> "Good Teacher, what must I do to inherit eternal life?" Jesus said to him, "Why do you call me good? No one is good but God alone. You know the commandments: 'You shall not commit adultery; You shall not murder; You shall not steal; You shall not bear false witness; Honor your father and mother.'" He replied, "I have kept all these since my youth." When Jesus heard this, he said to him, "There is still one thing lacking. Sell all that you own and distribute the money to the poor, and you will have treasure in heaven; then come, follow me." But when he heard this, he became sad; for he was very rich." (Luke 18:18–23)

These meetings have a very intimate personal character. But there is also a striking and constant concern for "those who are far away." More precisely, they are "far away from everything." They include sinners, the "unclean" and lepers, as well as the little ones and the poor of all types. They are "country folk," the masses of the little people, the marginalized and those neglected by all the elites. Jesus declares that he has come as much for them as for anyone else. The Aramaic expression *am-ha-aretz*, literally designates the "people of the countryside/earth." They were denigrated and despised by the Pharisees because of their inability—usually due to their work—to satisfy the legislative code of "purity." Remember, this purity notion is legal and cultural more than moral and spiritual. Uncleanness resulted notably, among other things, from eating forbidden foods, from working in forbidden professions, such as publicans, or associating with those who do, from failing to perform required ritual ablutions and the like.

On this theme of the relationships or social "network" of Jesus, we can conclude with two brief notes. On the one hand, we must note that Jesus came for a mission that had to be recognized as universal. Nonetheless, for all practical purposes, Jesus never left the Palestine of his day. One day, therefore, the question will inevitably be raised about the future of the mission and its means! Furthermore, the evangelical narrative repeatedly shows Jesus withdrawing far from the crowds and even away from his disciples, in silence and prayer—more precisely still: into intimacy with the one he calls his Father (Matt 14:23; Mark 6:45–46; Luke 3:21). One way or another we must clarify the nature of that relationship too.

How did Jesus see death? How did he see it in relation to himself?

Destiny confronts every human being, and we have already underlined the fact that Jesus obviously did not escape it. The question is therefore raised about how he saw it for himself, and what he said to others about it. How did this wise man think about this subject which naturally concerned him in the first place? How could this sage remain silent on a theme that concerns everyone?

It is already clear that when he began his public activity, he enjoyed great success with the "crowds." This was quickly followed by a lack of interest and then by hostility. He also attracted suspicion and eventually declared enmity on the part of both religious and political officials. Jesus had to be fully conscious that his "case" would end badly. The gospel presentation of the way in which he decided to "go up to Jerusalem" already makes that clear. Several times along the route to the capital with his disciples, he warned them that they had to expect adversity not only for him but for them as well. He went so far as to sharply rebuke Peter who did not want to hear that information: "Get behind me, Satan!" (Mark 8:33).

How can you explain his clear premonition and his disciples' refusal to accept it?

The reason is a persistent ambiguity. While Jesus clearly saw his mission on the uniquely spiritual level of the kingdom of God, the disciples and the crowds wanted to hear nothing about that, let alone accept it. Many ended up leaving his company. As for those who grasped the exclusively spiritual nature of his message, namely the cultic and religious leaders, they found in that message the primary reason for their own hostility toward him. To them he appeared more and more like a competitor. They also feared that the political powers would feel threatened. In either case, they were concerned about the danger of public disturbances. The French singer/songwriter Guy Béart saw as much when he sang, with reference to John 11:50: "Pilate was right after all / there was no need to kill them all, let just one man take the fall."

Faced with a growing threat of death, Jesus could have relied on what he and the people of the God of Abraham, Isaac, and Jacob believed and hoped for, and what he himself had even taught to all his listeners. But he was "fully human" and that hope could not keep him from being overwhelmed by physical pain and the pangs of death. That pain becomes clear to us when we read the gospel accounts of the drama from the agony in the Garden of Gethsemane, through the trial, and all the way to the cross.

Obviously, the tragedy of the Passion of Jesus, for that is what we call the long journey from his condemnation to his death on the cross, deeply marked those who followed him after those events. The writers of these gospel texts sought to cast light on the terrible mystery that the end of the life of Jesus seemed to represent to them. They did so by appealing to statements they found in the Old Testament. One such reference is Isaiah's poetic song of the "Servant of Yahweh," whose tragic destiny would be the source of redemption and blessing for the multitudes. They also appealed to the lamentation psalms in which the just man cries out to Yahweh, his God, in his distress and hope.

And how did his life come to an end?

Eventually rebuked and rejected, the culminating point of the confrontation with distress that the preacher, wonder-worker, and exorcist Jesus must have foreseen as his end, finds its clear expression in the cry he emitted from the cross. It is taken from Psalm 22: "My God, my God, why have you forsaken me?" (Mark 15:34). We can hardly doubt that there is something authentic here. How could the disciples, concerned with bearing witness to the divinity of Jesus in writing their story—how could they have invented such a statement that seems so unsuitable in promoting their cause? (Is this not another example of "the criterion of difference"?)

These final facts confront us with an unavoidable question. How can we understand the identity of someone who demonstrated throughout his earthly existence such a profound sense of God and such noble humanity, and yet at the end of his life was faced with the most horrible trials in almost total isolation and deepest darkness? Moreover, he seems to have been entirely abandoned by the very one he had always counted on.

However, Jesus will not collapse or revolt. He will find the strength to address in prayer the One in whom he had total confidence; the One who at the moment when everything should have been resolved, appears to have abandoned him pitilessly. For the cry of distress Jesus uttered as he was about to die: "My God, my God, why have you forsaken me," I say it again, this cry is a prayer, because it is addressed to God himself.

3

IDENTITY

In your account we can see that Jesus was an exceptional individual, but he did not escape the ordinary lot of every human being. So, don't we have to think of him as simply another man? He was undoubtedly an exceptional man and an eminent master of wisdom. However, all things considered, isn't he much like Socrates, especially in his way of facing death?

Indeed, it is not unreasonable to think about Socrates when we are trying to understand the identity of Jesus.

We have already examined similarities between Jesus and a true master of wisdom. That is already enough to make us think of Jesus in relation to great philosophical figures like Plato, Aristotle, and others who have handed down their reflections and teaching to us. But there are specific reasons for associating Socrates and Jesus. Our cultural history owes much to both. Both were condemned to death, the highest witness of their commitment to the wisdom each of them taught in his own way. They were both indicted for casting doubt on the concept of God or divinity that was dominant among their contemporaries. Because of that they were seen as subverting the social order. They both preferred to die rather than be untrue to themselves. That fact earned for them the admiration of at least many of their followers.

However, there are significant differences between these

two esteemed personalities. On the one hand, much of what Socrates taught shows his predominant concern about the political government of the city. We find nothing of the sort in the message of Jesus. On the other hand, and much more significantly, the great Athenian philosopher makes no mention of a God who is Father; nor does he speak of the human hope for salvation.

Finally, there is a dramatic difference in the way the two men died. On his deathbed, Socrates calmly continued teaching his disciples as he imbibed the hemlock that would slowly take his life. Jesus, who was delivered over to torture in virtual solitude, loudly conveys his physical pain and psychological distress. How can we understand this?

What can we say about the identity of Jesus? In the end, who was he?

In fact, although a great thinker like Erasmus (ca. 1469–1536) could speak about a genuine "philosophy of Christ," Jesus seems to fit much more naturally into the line of Jewish prophecy—the line of those who *speak* "in the place and in the name of God"—rather than in the Greek philosophical tradition. We might start, for example, by referring to the question Jesus himself addresses to his disciples in Mark: "'Who do people say that I am?' And they answered him, 'John the Baptist; and others, Elijah; and still others, one of the prophets'" (8:27–28). It is rather clear: whenever someone in the company of Jesus raised the question about his identity, they spontaneously looked in the direction of prophecy for the answer. Already John the Baptist seemed to fit in this category, and Jesus seems to have approved of that way of understanding him. Jesus himself questions his disciples about the Baptist: "What did you go out into the wilderness to look at? A reed shaken by the wind? What then did you go out to see? Someone dressed in soft robes? Look, those who wear soft robes are in royal palaces. What then did you go out to see? A prophet? Yes, I tell you, and more than a prophet" (Matt 11:7–9). There we hear clearly, "more than one prophet among others." This will be confirmed in what follows.

As for Elijah, the great biblical prophet who is mentioned here along with John the Baptist, he was still very much remembered in that time as the one who was carried off to heaven in a "chariot of fire," without dying. They awaited his return as a decisive event in the history of salvation. So, it is hardly surprising that some people began to wonder if Jesus was the hoped-for return of the ancient prophet!

Moreover, when Jesus began his public life, at the time that the Baptist was exercising his ministry, there was no shortage of "prophets" and "messiahs." They claimed to work the kinds of "signs and wonders" that Moses did when he obtained the manna (Exod 16:1–15) and led the chosen people dry-shod across the Red Sea (Exod 14:15–31), or the deeds that Joshua accomplished when he turned the Jordan River back so that the people could pass into the promised land. In Jesus's day each of the new "prophets" claimed to be the "long-awaited prophet of the last days." It is very revealing that before John the Baptist disappeared (Matt 14:3–12), he sent emissaries to Jesus asking the same question about his identity: "Are you the one who is to come, or are we to wait for another?" (Matt 11:3). For good measure, we can finally point out the fact that, in the days following the departure of Jesus, the well-known disciples on the road to Emmaus[1] spoke of him as "a prophet mighty in deed and word" (Luke 24:19). They were echoing in some way the feeling expressed by "the crowds" when Jesus entered Jerusalem on Palm Sunday[2] several days before his passion: "This is the prophet Jesus from Nazareth in Galilee" (Matt 21:11).

If Jesus is a prophet, how is he different from the others? After all, he does not seem to be presented in a different way, does he?

It is difficult to think that the word *prophet* is the best or most adequate word to define Jesus. In fact, those who continued speaking about him after his death quickly replaced this designation with other titles; undoubtedly, they found that term too imprecise to capture his personality. Because of what was so surprising and even disturbing in his teaching and his behavior, the question itself remained vague. A prophet? Perhaps, and in the end, he was at least that: had he not spoken in the name of God? But what sort of prophet? His followers had to come to an agreement, and they still must: such an identification is too ambiguous.

Jesus uses the term *prophet* when speaking about himself. Therefore, this designation is not totally inappropriate in his case. But it is also true that he only applies it to himself *indirectly* and that fact raises questions. Thus, in Mark 6:4 we read, "Then Jesus said to them, 'Prophets are not without honor, except in their hometown'"; and in Luke 13:33, he said, "It is impossible for a prophet to be killed outside of Jerusalem." Obviously, this is not the last word. We must continue examining this question.

How did Jesus present himself?

We might think that right from the beginning Jesus had nothing more urgent or more important to do than enlighten his followers about what or who he thought he was and was in truth. Would not that have been the right way to have his words and deeds accepted, dispelling any ambiguity about the matter of his title and authority with the positions he was taking? No, not at all! Jesus never proceeded that way. He consistently refused to accept the titles the crowds successively tried to pin on him throughout his public life.

The title *Christ* is the best example of his reticence about titles. In Mark's Gospel, Jesus had just asked his disciples in the clearest possible way ("Who do people say that I am?"), and most of them gave the kind of answer we have already seen: "John the Baptist; and others, Elijah; and still others, one of the prophets." Peter then spoke up solemnly in the name of the group and declared, "You are the Christ" (RSV). Jesus reacts by giving them the following command: "He sternly ordered them not to tell anyone about him" (Mark 8:27–30).

Now, this example is not an isolated incident. Following the gospel step by step, we get the impression that Jesus is constantly in retreat mode. Still, toward the end of his life, the gospel account clearly shows traces of the evangelists' discomfort in presenting the attitude of Jesus. It appeared very problematic to them. In fact, in Mark's Gospel, when Jesus responds to the high priest's question, "Are you the Messiah, the Son of the Blessed One?" he answers, "I am" (14:61–62). In Matthew's account, the response is "You have said so" (Matt 26:64). Curiously, in Mark's Gospel that will also be the way Jesus answers Pilate's question: "Are you the king of the Jews?" (Mark 15:2).

Did Jesus have a precise reason for maintaining this mystery about his identity?

No matter how the question of his identity is posed, everything happens as if he refused to take a position on this subject. Or rather, he wanted to make it clear to the person raising the question that it was up to that person to provide a reply. In any case, the impression Jesus wants to give is that no one will come to any clarity about his identity if they think in terms of preestablished categories; that is, if they try to associate him with figures that are already well known. And he frequently warns his disciples that they "cannot yet" understand what he is all about. They will have to accompany him further, and things will become clear later.

In other words, Jesus says what he has to say and does what he must do, without worrying too much, at least at first, about the effect it can have on those around him. All that will happen to him will eventually provide the answer to questions about his identity and provide the proper way to understand it. In the meantime, he is content just "to be there," so to speak. As the Gospels repeat regularly, "Let anyone with ears to hear listen" (Mark 4:23; see also Matt 11:15).

King, Messiah, or something else; he never took a clear position. Did he ever identify himself with a title?

In fact, he did occasionally give himself a title, and it is even more striking that he is the only one to use it: "Son of Man." Now, far from resolving the question, this title raises it once again, since its meaning appears complex.

It is a "semitism," that is, an expression current at the time, which does not necessarily represent a title but simply a way of designating oneself—as if he was called "a son of a man" or "a human being"; or more simply "myself" or "I" (see, for example, Matt 8:20: "The Son of Man has nowhere to lay his head"). However, this expression also calls to mind an earlier biblical passage from chapter 7 of the Book of Daniel. In contrast to what has just been said, the "Son of Man" is used there for the transcendent figure of the "Judge of the last days" appearing on "the clouds of heaven" (v. 13, RSV). Here again, however, the identification is unclear, as Mark indicates: "Those who are ashamed of me and of my words in this adulterous and sinful generation, of them the Son of Man will also be ashamed when he comes in the glory of his Father with the holy angels" (8:38). The formulation can be surprising, but the idea is at least that we have not heard the final word about the Son of Man and about what happened to him in the course of history.

He belongs to the human condition with the limits and trials that necessarily mark that condition. But he also claims a mysterious and transcendent judicial authority. Therefore, no one can expect Jesus himself to resolve the questions he (occasionally) poses or (finally) raises by the entirety of his behavior and destiny. It is everyone's responsibility to find an answer to that question.

Therefore, in the end we are obliged to "interpret" the identity of Jesus, because it is not self-evident. Is that it?

If we settle for speaking about Jesus as a preacher, as a wonder-worker or exorcist, as a wise man and a sage, and even as a philosopher or a prophet, we are working at a level of understanding accessible to anyone and distinct from any faith commitment. However, the famous movement of the search for the historical Jesus at the end of the nineteenth century and the beginning of the twentieth century has made it clear that no one can arrive at a completely objective and definitive interpretation of Jesus. It will always be dependent on the seeker's vision of the world and the understanding of human existence that the person brings to the subject of that inquiry. Put more simply, when we do historical research, we are not only interpreting, but we have always already interpreted. That is so not only in the case of Jesus, but for any and every historical person and event, whether we are talking about Socrates, Alexander the Great, Napoleon, or the French Revolution.

As for Jesus, the difficulty is that different interpretations about his identity may already have been proposed not only during his lifetime, but also in the years following his departure and even right up to our own time. Surprisingly, there have always been interpretations that include a properly *transcendent* dimension and hold an essential place in the New Testament texts that pertain directly and explicitly to Jesus. This means that *Jesus is only presented to us in a collection of unified literary documents, the Gospels and the entire New Testament, that provides most of the historical data about him! All these documents clearly present him to us as "more than simply Jesus."*

No one is obliged to accept this data as historical if they do not have the means of confirming it. But for all that, no one has the authority to affirm a priori that it has no relevance or meaning! The question of access to the identity of Jesus requires a method. Treating it adequately presupposes articulation of trustworthy criteria in order to come to a decision about it.

All of that does indeed cast light on why those who are interested in Jesus, during his lifetime and thereafter, have been driven to make declarations about him and proclaim his identity even at the risk of their lives, if we can put it that way. Does that explain the fact that he was designated and proclaimed by titles like Messiah, Son of God, and Lord?

Looking closely, we can see that a relatively large number of titles were attributed to Jesus in the New Testament. They vary according to the communities or the groups that speak about him: Master (or Rabbi), Son of David, King of the Jews (according to the Synoptic Gospels); or the Holy One, the Righteous One, the Servant (according to Acts 3:12–14); or again the Shepherd or Pastor (John's Gospel). However, in the end, three titles dominate: Christ, Son of God, and Lord. These are the ones we must examine.

We will begin with *Christ*. We have already noted that this title ended up being almost systematically attached to the name of Jesus in the expression "Jesus Christ." This was so much the case that people soon forgot that the two terms remain distinct. We must insist on this point: if the first term denotes the proper name of the man of Nazareth, the second is, properly speaking, a title. That title designates an honor and a function. The one *named* Jesus is *called*, confessed, and recognized as the Christ, that is, the Messiah, since "Christ" is simply the Greek translation of the Hebrew word for "Messiah." To say of Jesus that he is the Christ, identifying him as Jesus Christ, is therefore no more and no less than recognizing that in him the long-awaited Messiah has come and has been revealed. This mysterious missionary was sent to represent God before his people, and to fulfill a mission of salvation in God's name![3]

A second major title attributed to Jesus is *Son of God*. At the beginning, it can convey a broad range of meanings. In the Bible, the expression can be applied to angels or used to designate the king or even the whole people of Israel; and toward the end of the Old Testament—just before Jesus and the Christian era—it could be applied to each member of that people. That can appear paradoxical because, at the same time, the title "Son of Man" came to be reserved for a single individual with a transcendent character, as we have already noted. In fact, we must acknowledge that Jesus never uses this title ("Son of God") to refer to himself. When the New Testament writings use it to express the conviction that Jesus is the proper, true, and only Son of God, it is more the result of his behavior and his entire destiny, rather than any declarations on his part, that he was recognized as such.

The third major title is *Kyrios/Lord*. Commonly used at the time of Jesus, it was also employed in a general sense, equivalent to our use of "sir." However, there is no doubt that in Paul and John we must recognize the name of God in that title, since he exercises in all things *Lordship par excellence*! The Letter to the Philippians clearly speaks in this way about "the name that is above every name" (2:9), and the Letter to the Colossians does not hesitate to affirm that "in him [Christ] the whole fullness of deity dwells bodily" (2:9)! The adversaries of Jesus made no mistake about that. According to John's Gospel, the trial will be based precisely on the accusation of blasphemy: "You, though only a human being, are making yourself God" (John 10:33).

But how did the disciples of Jesus, and particularly the apostles, come to apply such titles to him, attributing to him a transcendent status in relation to the human condition, and even a divine status?

Here we must be clear: they did it and were driven to do it because they were firmly convinced that Jesus was *risen*; he had definitively passed through death! That is the one and only reason why the apostles were led to recognize and announce that he was this Christ-Messiah, this Son of God, and this Lord we have just described. The question that arises from this point forward is therefore knowing what led them to profess that their master was risen.

Since the resurrection is a point that has marked history, it directly concerns the Jesus of history. This is therefore not only nor entirely a matter of faith. The historical-critical method of exegesis offers some valuable elements for reflection.[4]

First, it is evident that after the death of Jesus his disciples were disheartened, dispersed, and demoralized. We can see that they found within themselves no energy to get anything going again without further developments concerning their master and his "cause."

The old rationalist argument affirmed that the disciples first concocted the story of the empty tomb and built the hypothesis of the resurrection of Jesus on that basis. Proponents of this argument then went on to say that this "hoax" then "duped people for the next twenty centuries." This argument is no longer plausible. It is ridiculous! Textual criticism has in fact established that the literary tradition[5] concerning the empty tomb and the literary tradition reporting the apparitions of Jesus after his death are totally independent. Therefore, we cannot pretend that the first was invented in order to prepare the way for the second.

Furthermore, it is also clear that the disciples were not in any way expecting what they announced as fact, at least not in the precise way that they proclaimed it. What they and the other children of Israel understood by the word *resurrection* corresponded to two types of events. It was either (1) the return of a deceased human being to his or her mortal existence, realizing that the person would eventually die again (this was the case for Lazarus, the friend of Jesus); or (2) a transformation of the entire universe coming after an apocalyptic conflagration at the end of time. Now the disciples announced a resurrection that (1) concerned only one individual, namely, Jesus; and (2) his resurrection introduced that unique human being to the properly eschatological (end of time) condition, quite apart from any universal transformation.

Therefore, we must ask what could have led the apostles to pass from total despondency after the death of Jesus to the confident proclamation of his resurrection understood in an astonishing new way. The answer is clear: when they explain what brought them to believe in an unheard-of event, they speak of experiences that we call the "appearances" of Jesus after his death. And so, the main question is really to draw out as much as possible what the apostles meant by the word *appearance*. To answer that question, the only possible method is critical analysis of the documents available to us, namely the New Testament "accounts of the Easter appearances."

What do these appearance accounts tell us?

After their master's death had completely disoriented them, the disciples of Jesus had the experience of reconnecting with him, of finding him alive again: in the course of a meal, on the road, by the lake; in other words, in situations that were familiar to them, but catching them totally off guard. Their dead master "presented himself alive to them." This way of expressing the events is very important. They did not say, "We have seen him (or "We have seen him again"), as we might expect, but "He was seen by us," and even: "He presented himself to be seen by us." It was certainly they who saw. But everything happened *for* them as if the initiative and even the operation of this "seeing" came entirely *from outside* of them: and precisely from him who "presented himself to be seen by them," "who gave himself to be seen by them," who "made them see him" (see Acts 1:3).

Thus, two factors allowed them to understand the very strange events that had "happened to them." First, they finally saw vindicated the hope that had sustained their life and the life of their entire people. Second, they came to see that what they had experienced with Jesus before his departure had definitively shed light on what they were experiencing so unexpectedly now.

What were the apostles hoping for? How could Jesus and his destiny, including these curious "appearances," have seemed to respond to their hopes?

The first of those who at Antioch, at some point during the years 40–50, were called "Christians" were Jews (see Acts

11:26). They were called "Jewish Christians," to distinguish them from the converts coming from the "Greek" or "pagan" culture. The latter group was growing quickly, thanks to Paul's three great "missionary journeys" in the Mediterranean. He passed through what is now Turkey, Greece, and the south of Italy, before reaching his final destination: Rome.

The first Christians were still professing the faith of the people of Israel. They were also waiting for God to send the Christ-Messiah who would bring them definitive deliverance in this world and in the next; in other words, salvation. Their hope reached its highest expression in the great cry of Isaiah: "O that you would tear open the heavens and come down" (64:1), and the question brought to Jesus by the disciples of John the Baptist: "Are you the one who is to come, or are we to wait for another?" (Matt 11:3). That was proof enough for them.

We must not lose sight of the fact that the attitude Jesus manifested in his words and deeds during his public ministry provided everything necessary to bring his companions to recognize that he was indeed the answer to the Baptist's question! Here are a few signs of that.

- ≈ It is certain that Jesus had already spoken in the following way on several occasions: "You have heard that it was said....But I say to you..." (Matt 5:21–22). Jesus therefore intended to give the same authority to his own word that the people and he himself accorded to the word of God.
- ≈ It is also certain that Jesus forgave sins (Mark 2:5–7). Now, if there is one prerogative in the Old Testament that no human being, not even the Messiah, could ever exercise, it is indeed the power to forgive people's sins. This is something that the Jewish faith always reserved for God alone.
- ≈ Once again, it is certain from the way in which Jesus addressed God, calling him "Abba" (Mark 14:36). Now

> we know that this term was not used by the believers of that time to speak about Yahweh their God. It was restricted to the domain of family relationships; it meant no more nor less than "papa." Moreover, we know that Jesus always carefully distinguished his own relationship with God from the relationship that his contemporaries maintained with God.

In addition, questions abounded around the figure of the prophet from Galilee. We need only mention a few passages from the Gospels to make the point, such as Mark 6:2–3: "Where did this man get all this? What is this wisdom that has been given to him? What deeds of power are being done by his hands!" One day Peter dared to resolve the question: "You are the Messiah, the Son of the living God" (Matt 16:16). However, it quickly became clear that he did not understand the real meaning of his own words. When Jesus went on to explain that the Messianic mission Peter attributed to him would lead to his death, Peter did not accept that teaching at all. This would be confirmed by what eventually followed (see John 18:15–27: Peter's denial of Jesus).

How does that explain the fact that the apostles came to proclaim Jesus as the Christ-Messiah, the Lord, the Son of God?

Jesus had certainly been recognized as "a prophet mighty in deed and word" (Luke 24:19). He had, nonetheless, been put to death. "But we had hoped that he was the one to redeem Israel" (Luke 24:21; see also Acts 1:6). Now, with the amazing Easter appearances, the questions were raised again! Did not what had already taken place before Golgotha get clarified by his reappearance after his death? Likewise, could not what had been so surprising about him in the days of his appearance in the flesh be cleared up by what now seemed to have happened to him beyond the grave? In short, did not what was so astonishing about him before Easter cast light on the equally astonishing events after Easter, and vice versa?

In any case, such was the passage to faith for the disciples. We must admit that they also made an act of faith! The amazing connection with the God that Jesus called his Father during his earthly life now seemed capable of conquering and passing through death itself. From that moment onward, it seemed normal to understand that Jesus rightly "belonged" to God. That in turn is verified in such a way that, within God, Jesus's entire self is joined to an "Other" from whom he is always receiving his existence and who appears from that moment onward as his Father.

Consequently, it became necessary henceforth to admit that there exists a Son in God—in other words, God does indeed have a Son who is just as divine as he is! Remember that the Jewish faith forbade his disciples from recognizing a man as God; in fact, his adversaries decided to put him to death precisely because they could not imagine such a blasphemous thought! But the resurrection changed everything, and those disciples could now arrive at a confession of faith and proclaim that Jesus, this prophet who was crucified by human hands but raised up by the power of God, was indeed himself God...or rather, more precisely, the Son of God.

Ultimately then, was the resurrection the determining factor in understanding the identity of Jesus in Christianity?

Having arrived at this point, yes, we can see just how much the Christian understanding of Jesus is linked to faith in his "resurrection from the dead" (Phil 3:11). Because he was believed and professed to be "risen," Christians came to recognize that there dwelt in him a power of life that could only come to him from the Master and Lord of all life, who is God alone. It was thus, *therefore*, that they could thereafter confess that Jesus belonged entirely to God himself—and hence his divinity, and in this sense, his Lordship as well.

However, his divinity and lordship are *received*. They are literally incarnated in him. Because these traits are always recognized and referred by Jesus to God whom he designates precisely as his Father, the "Lord-God" that Jesus himself also was, had to be seen, strictly speaking, as the "*Son* of God."

Now it was clear that he was not only God who came forth as Son from the Father but also that he was "sent by the Father," "from the Father's presence," as we read in the first verse of the Gospel of John. It is in his very quality of true Lord and true Son of God that the title of Messiah-Christ could correctly be applied to him. This Messiah, in the tradition of the chosen people, designated the transcendent figure whose sending by God was long awaited and on whom were concentrated all the hopes of the believing children of Israel.

Son of God, Lord, Christ-Messiah: these three titles are closely bound to faith in the resurrection of Jesus. For Christians, therefore, was Jesus at one and the same time man—and therefore subject to death—and God?

Yes, and what we have just said demonstrates that, as well as why Christians were led to believe that Jesus must finally be recognized as both "true God" and "true man." His death had made his full humanity clear. But a further result was that Christians learned important truths not only about Jesus, but also about God and humanity.

First, about God. They quickly realized that if God is only God in having a Son, and if however, he is not divided (otherwise he would not be God!), it is because the bond that unites the Father to the Son and the Son to the Father—namely, this Spirit that the Gospel of John speaks about—also participates himself in their divinity in making them one. Therefore, Christians came to confess that the God who revealed himself in Jesus is not "only God," but "one and the same God," precisely as Father, Son, and Holy Spirit.

Next, regarding humanity: Christians understood that if in Jesus God has indeed revealed himself, this cannot be understood as unintentional on his part, nor is it without implications for the human race, to whom he came by and in Jesus. Therefore, the question arises, why and for what did he come? The reply is explicitly formulated by the Creed that Christians still profess: He became man "for us and for our salvation."

But Jesus is not only recognized as "risen"; he is professed and proclaimed as "Savior." What does this title mean, and how can Jesus be a savior? More fundamentally, what can "salvation" mean for humanity?

Salvation: now that is a big word. We certainly must explain that one![6]

≈ First of all, salvation *from what*? We can refer here to a formula used by Jesus himself. Some were amazed that he had healed a paralytic sinner; they thought it was not appropriate for a "man of God" to ignore the "proper people" in "good social circles" and reach out instead to the marginalized, despised, and excluded, even respecting and helping them. Jesus replied, "Know that the Son of Man has authority on earth to forgive sins" (Mark 2:10; see also Luke 19:10; Matt 15:24; 10:6). He closes the episode of his encounter with the chief tax collector Zacchaeus saying, "The Son of Man came to seek out and to save the lost" (Luke 19:10). It could not be clearer, and everyone can understand it (even if they do not believe it!). Salvation and, therefore, the savior who brings it are indicated precisely because they reclaim the lost from perdition. They are revealed in the fact that one who was lost is "found again," that one who was heading for death is reborn and lives again.

Naturally, the life in question is the life of the entire human being, body and soul, heart and mind; if it were not so, it would not be salvation of the person! The evil and death in question here are both bodily and spiritual. The great liturgical Litanies, chanted during the most solemn celebrations of the Church asking God for "deliverance," include the following petitions: "From all sin and from every evil, deliver us, O Lord" and later "From death deliver us, O Lord!" Along with what we are delivered from by salvation, we can be clear about *why* we are delivered. It concerns a victory of life where there was death, of happiness where there was suffering and evil, of holiness and grace where there was alienation from God and sin. On a more positive note, at the heart of it all we can sum it up in the idea of fullness of life, in a community of grace with God himself.

≈ Salvation *how*, then? Starting from the moment when God takes the initiative, in Jesus, to send his own Son to earth and into human history to establish and reestablish communication with humanity, the covenant is definitively sealed, the way is opened, and the bridge is built between God and the human family. In the course of the centuries, many formulas have been used to describe this event, but they all express the same faith and the same conviction: in Jesus life has conquered death on its own terrain; the possibility of forgiveness has been decreed for every fault and every sin; and "the grace of God has [definitively] appeared" (Titus 2:11).

≈ Finally, salvation *for whom*? What we have just explained indicates that the salvation opened by Jesus is offered to all humanity and to each of its members. The only condition will be that they are open to receive it, really and freely available to welcome it in whatever way they can; that is, in accordance with the way they live and understand their existence in this world. For the God who wanted them to be free would never in any way constrain them afterward, even to bestow on them his best gifts.

Christian theologians strive to clarify the "openness" in question here:

≈ It is best realized where the recognition of Jesus Christ as Savior is professed explicitly, celebrated sacramentally,[7] and lived existentially.

≈ It presupposes the following: renouncing self-sufficiency and egocentrism; corresponding openness to the other and through him to the "Other" that "people call God." And in all that, readiness to allow total trust to develop within. When all is said and done, this is certainly possible.

Therefore, no one can be a priori excluded from the salvation offered by the one who is revealed in Jesus Christ as the God of all human beings. We can reasonably believe that people outside the first group just mentioned, namely Christian believers, can have access to it. Those who are striving to the best of their ability to live according to the second type of "openness," in their souls and consciences, those we call "people of good will," may also receive this gift.

How can we understand the fact that this Son of God and Savior had to undergo humiliation, the cross, and death?

That question arises naturally after all that has just been said. We surely understand at this point that Jesus died because the civil authority of his day condemned him to the death reserved for those who disturbed the political or religious order. Nonetheless, we cannot help asking how valid this explanation is, when we discover that Jesus was not only sent by God, but that he is God's own Son who came and was "incarnate" in our human condition.

Must we, or can we, therefore, offer the suggestion that it is God himself who would have wanted and even willed such a destiny for his Christ? In any case, Paul dared to say so, for he does indeed declare that "he [God] did not withhold his own Son" (Rom 8:32). In doing so he echoes the surprising passages in the Gospels where Jesus warns his disciples of the fate that awaits him. Even more startling, the conclusion we must come to is that Jesus did not simply consent to his own death but willed it: "For this reason the Father loves me, because I lay down my life in order to take it up again. No one takes it from me, but I lay it down of my own accord" (John 10:17–18; see also 13:1).

Must we then understand that the death of Jesus on the cross corresponds to the divine will? In that case, Pilate and the others would only have served as unwitting instruments of God's plan. This means that the cross of Jesus and the God who willed it rise to the level of what is called a "great Mystery." We are therefore dealing with something entirely beyond understanding.[8]

Surely, then, the question must be posed: "But *who, then, is this God,* who chose to reveal himself in such a disturbing way?" Are those who hold his existence to be self-evident out of line in the way they speak about him?

This has been the response of Christian faith. Yes, certainly, God must be powerful, and even all-powerful. If not, he would no longer be God! However, his power is of an entirely different order than what we ourselves usually consider "power," for example, the power and means of power furnished by money, political domination over one's contemporaries, accompanied by prestige, success, and honors for the one exercising power. The power of God would therefore be purely and simply the power of love: love that is *only* love; love that is consenting and given; love that is generous and gratuitous; love that implies selflessness, that puts the other in first place. In the end, *that is what it really means* to be powerful, and even all-powerful!

And so, the cross would not only be understood as an infamous punishment and atrocious torture?

The meaning of the cross and death of Jesus is turned upside down, so to speak. It would no longer be just a horribly painful punishment inflicted by the human reaction of rejection and the power of condemnation. On the contrary, it is a mysterious power that is ultimately capable of claiming victory over the people who had pretended to dominate and subject everything. In no way is it a sign of resignation and capitulating weakness. On the contrary, it is a sign of an unprecedented, mysterious wisdom, definitively reversing what worldly wisdom, science, and power had appeared to impose.

In any case, that is what Christians dared to see in the cross and death of Jesus Christ, revised in the light of his resurrection. We must insist on this point: it is the central element and even the criterion of their faith—so much so, that they chose the "sign of the cross" as their distinctive badge. And it is clear, or it surely ought to be clear, that if it had not gone that way, there would never have been either Christians or Christianity.

We will come back to the fact that, in the course of history, disciples of Jesus lost sight of that original choice on the part of the Father and Jesus. Nevertheless, Paul's message continued to be transmitted from generation to generation: "We proclaim Christ crucified, a stumbling block to Jews and foolishness to Gentiles....I decided to know nothing among you except Jesus Christ, and him *crucified*" (1 Cor 1:23; 2:2).

> Though he was in the form of God,
> [he] did not regard equality with God
> as something to be exploited,
> but emptied himself,
> taking the form of a slave,
> being born in human likeness.
> And being found in human form,
> he humbled himself
> and became obedient to the point of death—
> even death on a cross.
>
> Therefore God also highly exalted him
> and gave him the name
> that is above every name.
>
> (Phil 2:6–9)

Do you think that message can still be received today?

I acknowledge that this question must be addressed. But in responding, I would like to pose another one. Are our contemporaries so confident that the scientific and technological discoveries and progress, the lights accumulated by triumphant reason in modernity and postmodernity, can or ever will enable them wisely to manage their prodigious progress and their resounding failures? What about their bottomless hunger for recognition and power? Can they really accept responsibility for the trials, the handicaps, and the miseries of so many of their brothers and sisters in the human family?

Such questions in response to yours are inevitably posed by the very existence of Jesus and those Christians who have followed him. Where is true "wisdom"? In the end, where is true "humanity"? Is it found where we only accept knowledge that is as critical and scientific as possible and where we cultivate an ever-growing desire for insatiable power, regardless of where and how that knowledge is deployed? Or is it found where there is more happiness in giving and in giving of oneself rather than in taking and possessing, in wisely accepting to arrive at consensus rather than always wanting to dominate?

Who can deny that to raise a child, to relieve heavy and very personal suffering, and to face so many questions that seem impossible from a human point of view, there is a greater "power" in the words and actions of love than in all the megatons of any other form of power? How can we hide from the truth that a society can only be and remain human if we find the means to help all the people who are marginalized and "excluded"? How can the human family escape from its concerns about economic prosperity if it wants to avoid total disaster for large segments of the population and ultimately the destruction of the entire planet?

If we can see the truth in those questions, what consequences can we draw that give true meaning to human life and resolve the question concerning "the one that people call God"? Christians are conscious of the choice they have made. Nevertheless, it is always possible that they have not always been and are still not always consistent in applying this choice concretely to their lives. Therefore, their "message" concerning the cross, the death, and the resurrection of Jesus Christ can be rendered less credible.

What realistic link is there between Jesus Christ and the Church, which is supposed to unite and bring together the Christians you have just mentioned?

Together we have discovered that Jesus came both to announce and to accomplish the work of salvation in human history. In accomplishing that work, he revealed himself and enabled his disciples to recognize him as God and more specifically as the Son of God. His mission had to include opening lines of communication with God, offering people God's own life and grace, capable of making them true "children of God." Adopted children, because they were enabled to participate in the full and unique childhood by the one who is the "Son par excellence." Christian tradition, which has been maintained and passed down since the first centuries of the common era, expresses that reality by saying that the disciples of Jesus the Christ can become "sons and daughters in the Son." They do so by receiving nothing more nor less than the Spirit who unites the Father and the Son and makes them one. In his Letter to the Galatians, Paul declares this truth in the clearest possible way: "God sent his Son, born of a woman, born under the law, in order to redeem those who were under the law, so that we might receive adoption as children" (4:4–5).

The identity of Jesus, the Prophet, Messiah, Son of God, and Savior, produces fruit that goes beyond the singular personality of Jesus and his own destiny, and in one way or another it concerns the entire human race. Every human being can participate, by God's grace and by adoption in this "Sonship," which properly belongs to Jesus Christ/the Son of God by his very nature. Saint Irenaeus (born around the year 140) did not hesitate to conclude that "if God became man," in Jesus, it was "so that human beings might become God."

Can we say in general that the fruit of the coming and destiny of Jesus is the Church? Is that why it is often presented as the "Body of Christ"?

In fact, this fruit was called to take the concrete form of an assembly. Jesus would be recognized as the Lord of this assembly for the precise reason that he made himself the servant of salvation for each of its members. Those who became his disciples across the centuries right up to our own time constitute that assembly:

≈ first, in responding by their effective conversion to the good news of the gospel of Jesus, the Son of God and Savior;

≈ then, by participating in the celebration of the sacraments by which they are effectively integrated into this community of believers;

≈ finally, by making the effort to carry forward and support, each in his or her own way, the message and the assembly of those who believe and celebrate the Christian faith.

This assembly is in fact what we call the Church. The Greek word *ekklēsia* for "Church" comes from the verb *kaleō*, which means "to call." Jesus Christ is considered not only the Savior of this assembly, but also the "shepherd" par excellence, or the "Good Shepherd" (John 10). There is another symbolic image that has the advantage of highlighting the organization of the various "functions" of those within the assembly. Jesus is presented as the "Head" of the Body and his disciples who gather around him are the members of that Body. From their union with their Head they receive their designation as Christians.

4

POSTERITY

If recognizing Jesus as Christ and Savior produced a community of "Christians," can we say that those who depended on him were distinct from him?

Without the slightest hesitation, the answer is *yes*. In fact, it is essential to distinguish between him and the community that followed him! It is important, as we just said, to honor the fact that we cannot separate his historical life, and therefore the personal identity of Jesus, from the fruit of his teaching, his actions, and his destiny. However, it is just as important to recognize that, while they are closely linked, the shepherd is not the flock, and the head is not the body. The Jesus *effect* is not the Jesus *fact*.

Remember the important distinction between *Jesus* and *Christ*. The first term, *Jesus*, designates the man of Nazareth who walked the roads of Palestine and died on the cross at Jerusalem. The second term, *Christ*, refers to the mysterious reality and the divine nature that carried forward the humanity of Jesus, that gave life to his entire historic existence, and that attached him so entirely to God that it made him God. Therefore, it is important to distinguish a divine element and a human element in "Jesus Christ." Christian tradition speaks here of the "two natures" of Jesus Christ, a divine nature on the one hand and a human nature on the other. However, while they are really distinct, they "function" in all things "without division or separation," because they are united in such a way as to constitute "one single and same person," who can really say "I." That Person is therefore capable of fully assuming a humanity like the humanity of each and every one of us, and is also capable of investing in the historical life and destiny of this individual human being all the dynamic existence of the only Son of God.

How can we distinguish the Church from Jesus if it is the Body of Christ?

The status of the Church is altogether different from the status of Jesus, and this is even more true with the status of Christianity as a whole. These must be understood as the entire institution and civilization that are attached to Jesus throughout the centuries. Neither of these is divine.

The Church itself, we must insist, is a purely human reality. The faith it professes and the sacraments it confers on its members give them access to the life of this God. They can become his children thanks to the way of salvation opened by Jesus Christ. This is a matter of pure grace, a totally gratuitous divine gift, whereas in Jesus the Christ we are talking about the properly divine dimension of his very being.

We must also add that, throughout the course of history, it has too often happened that members of Christ's Church, including those responsible for that community, have "betrayed their Master." Some, like Judas (see Matt 10:4; Mark 3:19; Luke 6:16), betrayed him. Others denied him. Peter did that, if only for a time; and he was the "first" among the apostles (see John 18:17–27). In addition, we must admit that, in the course of the twenty centuries that have led up to our own times, there have been too many demonstrations of triumphalism and too many compromises with public authorities. Furthermore, clerical attitudes have often tried to control mindsets, if not consciences! The ambiguity of the word *crusades* can provide a striking example here.[1] The first intention was to liberate the Holy Sepulcher (the site of Jesus's burial) from threats posed by the Muslim occupation of the city. Unfortunately, a belligerent spirit of reconquest and declared hostility led to terrible abuses that ended up seriously compromising the whole venture.

But Christianity cannot be reduced to the Church! Can it?

What we mean by the word *Christianity* has conveyed a set of values, traits that constitute a great civilization and spirit, a stream of representations, and finally a vision of the world. These elements have increasingly tended to lose their connection with the Christian inspiration that gave them birth. It can even be said that many have completely lost sight of the Christian origin of these values. They include, for example, recognition of the undeniable value of every human being; the affirmation of the primacy of love and of service in all human behavior; the a priori positive appreciation of all created reality ("and God saw that it was good"); and the idea that history is not an endless repetition nor an inescapable descent into decadence, but a living dynamic linking the future with progress.

Even in the face of deliberate attempts to cause division and betrayal, the message of the gospel about Jesus, his teaching, his deeds, and his destiny has continued to be passed on. The message itself has provided and continues to provide criteria by which to judge, to criticize, and to denounce anything in the Church that is false to the name of Christian. History gives us the names of many saints who have done just that. At the same time, many Christian institutions, even at their worst, have not failed to transmit the message. That message itself provides all that is needed to confront them and their identity with what they received from their founder.

Clearly, there is a difference between Jesus Christ and all that has followed him. Nonetheless, it is a fact that among his disciples some individuals have responsibility to speak and act in his name, to represent him in some way. Under what title and with what authority do they do so?

A New Testament document bearing the title "The Letter to the Hebrews," written sometime between the years AD 80 and 90, presents Jesus as the "one mediator between God and humankind" (1 Tim 2:5). We are invited to understand that he is the only individual in human history to be both God and man. We are also taught that the salvation he came to make available to us is offered to all human beings. Now, the "uniqueness" of Jesus Christ in his personal identity and his meaning for the salvation of the human race is not only relevant to those who have not yet benefited from his salvation. It also applies to the Christian assembly itself, in the heart of the Church constituted by those who have become Christians! Nothing and no one in this Church can ever come forward to compete with the role of Jesus the Christ, nor could they ever replace him. Everything that is received, experienced, and promoted by Christians is "through him and with him and in him," as the closing words of the great Eucharistic Prayer of the Mass tell us.

The pope is not the successor of Jesus, but of Peter, who was neither another Jesus nor another Christ, but the one sent by Jesus Christ, that is, an apostle, and he is Christ's representative, but only *up to a certain point.* After all, he himself is subject to the sole Lordship of Jesus the Christ. And if it is that way with Peter and all his successors, it is even more so for those other envoys, representatives, and/or "ministers" of the Church who bear the title of bishop, priest, or deacon.

Admittedly, we must acknowledge that within the institutional apparatus of the Catholic Church, and especially among its leaders, some have yielded to the temptations of clericalism and even triumphalism. These "churchmen" have sometimes been inclined to present themselves as the only ones who possess the truth and deserve to be recognized as such. But that does not come from Jesus and it does not represent the mission received from him. Therefore, it should always be denounced. That is precisely what happened, for example, with Saint Francis of Assisi and Saint Catherine of Siena; both challenged the popes of their respective times. This was certainly part of the message of the Catholic hierarchy at the Second Vatican Council (1962–65). It has always inspired and still does inform the attitude and the interventions of Pope Francis in our day.

If they are representatives of Jesus, in what sense can we say that the ministers of the Church can speak and act in his name? Do they judge the conformity of Christians to the message of Jesus? What is their role?

The ministers of the Church are not expected to teach their own ideas, nor a truth or a perspective on things that they themselves have constructed based on Jesus's teaching or any other source. They are to teach the gospel of Jesus the Christ, and they are first expected to adhere and conform themselves to his gospel. If they can claim that they confer grace and ultimately the life of God by the sacraments they celebrate with those who come to receive them, they are also always obliged to receive them for themselves. They are only at the service of the communication of this life in as much as it comes from an "Other" who is God. This life is brought about through them in other people who surrender not to them but to God. Finally, on that basis, these ministers of the Church have a duty to gather the human family, to guide and govern the community of disciples regarding the order of faith. At the same time, they must always respect the freedom of those who receive the message, with the goal of maintaining the unity of all believers, and of all people insofar as that is possible.

Teaching doctrine, celebrating the sacraments, exercising "pastoral" responsibility: whatever their rank, the representatives and ministers of the Church are called to exercise their ministry precisely in these three domains. They can authentically claim to represent Jesus only if they present themselves as performing a service that falls under these ministries[2] and is beneficial to people's lives.

In the seventeenth century, Bishop Jacques-Bénigne Bossuet of Meaux, France, could say that the Church is "Jesus Christ extended and communicated." We must certainly understand all the same that no one who comes after Jesus Christ in the Church is justified in claiming to be his substitute in any way. Therefore, it is only under the very precise conditions and modalities that I have just described intentionally that the ministers of the Church are called and authorized to "represent" him.

We have just been discussing the relation between Jesus and what followed him, the succeeding generations. Has that relation evolved over the centuries? Can you describe the stages of development?

In any case it is important to place in a special category what we call the "apostolic generation." Only those who spent time with Jesus "in the days of his flesh" (Heb 5:7) and who saw him again after his resurrection could give eyewitness testimony about him. They were the only ones who had immediate contact with the one whose life, death, and resurrection are at the foundation and the heart of the Christian faith. This is how the author of the First Letter of Saint John saw things: "We declare to you what was from the beginning, what we have heard, what we have seen with our eyes, what we have looked at and touched with our hands...we declare to you what we have seen and heard so that you also may have fellowship with us" (1 John 1:1–3).

That is also why, regarding the resurrection of Jesus, we have already stated that we are relying on the "apostolic witness." The Creed we still use every Sunday in Catholic worship confesses that the Church can only be "one, holy, [and] catholic" if it is also "apostolic."

For a relatively brief period—one or two generations—those who professed faith in him, without ever encountering him in person, could still refer to those predecessors who had met him. Thus, they could consult the eyewitnesses when they had questions about him. We have a good example in what the evangelist Luke wrote in the introduction to his own "testimony": "Since many have undertaken to set down an orderly account of the events that have been fulfilled among us, just as they were handed on to us by those who from the beginning were eyewitnesses and servants of the word, I too decided, *after investigating everything carefully from the very first*, to write an orderly account for you, most excellent Theophilus, so that you may know the truth concerning the things about which you have been instructed" (Luke 1:1–4).

How and by what means could they continue to refer to Jesus after the time of the direct witnesses, and then in the time after those who had known these witnesses?

From the beginning of the second century after Jesus Christ, no one could any longer offer a personal recollection of Jesus during the time of his earthly existence and up to the time of his death. So, how did they proceed when new questions were raised about him? The questions raised at this point were newer and more difficult to deal with in the decade spanning the years

40 to 50. By that time, thanks to the missionary efforts of Saint Paul and others, the Church was expanding beyond Jewish territory, where the faith had first been planted. By this time the followers of Jesus were proclaiming the Christian faith to Greek society and culture.

Historians of Christian doctrine have demonstrated that in the early centuries (from the second to the seventh century), whenever a question about Jesus was raised, they proceeded to resolve it by resorting to arguments based on the question of salvation. They relied on what had been handed down during the earlier period concerning his life, death, and resurrection, and ultimately concerning the recognition of his divine sonship. And they always chose the response that seemed the best to guarantee the salvation of the human family. After all, they had discovered that this was why he came in the first place.

For example, in the context of the gnostic[3] threat to the faith, some questioned whether Jesus had a "real body." In answering this question, they surely relied on the testimony of those who spoke of what they had "heard, seen, and touched." Church leaders went on to affirm that if he only had what "appeared" to be a body, the salvation he brought would in no way concern the human body but only the "soul" or "spirit." Now it is essential from the Christian-biblical perspective to affirm the salvation of the body, because that is essential to human identity as such. They therefore had to conclude that unless salvation includes the body it would not really be salvation.

They took the same approach when the question was raised about the unity of Jesus. Since he was both true God and true man, was he "truly *one*"? The answer was yes, provided that there remained in him a true "distinction without separation" of the divine and the human.

Such debates are called "Christological" because they are

about Jesus precisely "as the Christ." They continued throughout the early centuries of the life of the Church, a period designated as the "Great Church Tradition." They were carried out by great theologians, mostly bishops, who are known as "Fathers of the Church." They include Ignatius of Antioch and Irenaeus of Lyons in the second century up to Isidore of Seville (636) for the Church in the West and John Damascene (749) for the East. Because of these debates a series of assemblies of bishops (called "ecumenical councils") were held. There are seven, including Nicaea (325) and Constantinople I (381), then Ephesus (431) and Chalcedon (451), and again Constantinople II (553), Constantinople III (680–81), and Nicaea II (787). They formulated clear responses (technically called "definitions") to the questions raised. The teaching of these ecumenical councils[4] was dedicated above all to defining Christian faith precisely concerning Jesus the Christ.

It is also significant that the first two of these councils agreed upon and approved a "symbol of faith" (that is, a definitive formulation of the faith). It was not changed[5] and has always remained in use at the Sunday celebration of the Mass (today it is called the "Nicene-Constantinopolitan symbol" or "Creed"). And it is also significant that these seven councils are recognized and professed by all the members of the various churches that were separated at later times: Orthodoxy (the separation came in 1454), and Protestantism (beginning in the sixteenth century with Martin Luther, John Calvin, and other theologians of the Protestant Reformation).

After this second great period, did questions of Christ's identity and message continue into the eighth century? Did references to Jesus Christ and his identity continue to develop and evolve?

The period that followed—let's say the beginning of the High Middle Ages—certainly brought forward many questions, discussions, and positions concerning Jesus the Christ. However, by that time the Church had passed beyond the New Testament Church, and beyond the "Great Church Tradition." In the period of the early Christian centuries, they had to explain the New Testament's message about Jesus, moving beyond its origins in the Jewish context into the vast and very different universe of Greek culture.

Theology continued to treat questions about Jesus throughout history. During the Middle Ages there developed scholastic theology.[6] Then there were the disputes and counterproposals of the Reformation and the Age of the Enlightenment. In the nineteenth century a new way of dealing with questions was made possible by the emergence of historical science. With that development it became necessary to redirect all theological reflection to new foundations. This in turn is what launched the dialogue in the present work, because that period has defined our own situation. Now we pose in our own day the question of "Jesus and Jesus Christ."

In the course of the centuries, when Christians called to mind the figure of Jesus it was not only an intellectual endeavor (by way of doctrines or dogmas). It was also aesthetic or artistic. How have those representations evolved over time?

In the early Christian era Jesus was not depicted in sculpted or painted images. This was undoubtedly a continuation of the Jewish tradition of prohibiting the creation of any sculpted image of Yahweh/God (Exod 20:4), since that would reduce him to the level of an "idol." It would also risk fostering superstitious practices. Instead, they used language, the written word, and music to express the mystery of God. And they addressed him in liturgical celebration with prayers of praise, supplication, and so on by way of psalms, hymns, and canticles (see Eph 5:19). These were supported by wind and string instruments of the day. Soon thereafter in the Eastern Orthodox tradition, there appeared the artform of the icon, conceived as a representation of the mysteries of the life of Christ and the saints. These images were considered worthy of veneration.

It was only toward the end of the third century that painted or sculpted artistic images of Jesus Christ began to appear. Rather discrete at first, their production quickly spread when a new form of Christian art appeared in architecture at the beginning of the fourth century.

Old resistance to images awakened and a movement called iconoclasm ("destruction of images") surfaced. It became such a widespread practice that a council (Nicaea II, the last of the seven ecumenical councils) assembled in order to deal with the problem. It condemned iconoclasm, pronounced in favor of icons, and prescribed appropriate ways of venerating them.

Given the tendency to prohibit representations of Jesus in the early Church, how can we explain the fact that images of him became so widespread?

There was a strong doctrinal motivation behind this development. Since Christian faith proclaimed the coming of the Son of God "in the flesh" and his incarnation in the world, it professed, as in the preface of the Eucharistic Prayer of the Mass for Christmas, that God, who by his nature is invisible, "made himself visible to our eyes." It holds that the words of Jesus were the words of God himself and the works of Jesus were the works of God himself. Thus, in responding to a question from his disciple Philip, Jesus could reply, "Whoever has seen me has seen the Father" (John 14:9). Yes, because it is expressed in this way, everything pushed that faith to represent in the various plastic arts the bodily figure of the "true man" that was Jesus, and to represent the many episodes in the life of "this man," who in his time could not only be heard but seen and even touched as well.

Are there general categories of the kinds of artistic representations of Jesus in the course of these two millennia "after Jesus Christ"?

That task would be immense. We will settle for identifying a few large types.

The beginnings are quite modest, and they appear in the Roman catacombs. There is a figure of a young shepherd, which appears to have been a favorite theme. But before long, there began to appear representations of the glory of the Risen Christ (we might mention the splendid mosaics of Ravenna and Monreale in the domes and tympana of the Byzantine churches along with the richness of Eastern Orthodox iconography: the *Pantocrator*, the Divine Majesty, and so on).

Throughout the Middle Ages the Church grew more and more attached to representations of the various mysteries of the life of Jesus with images depicting scenes from the Gospels, from the annunciation and nativity all the way to the appearances of the Risen Christ. In the fourteenth and fifteenth centuries there was a strong emphasis on what we might call the true humanity of Jesus the Christ. This was expressed with an abundance of images depicting the sufferings of his passion: the condemnation, the flagellation, the way of the cross, the crucifixion, and so on.

Many artists put their efforts to the task of presenting the human and divine mystery of the unique personality of Jesus, from Giotto and Fra Angelico to Rembrandt, passing by way of Mantegna and El Greco.

Coming to the modern and contemporary periods of art, interest was directed to the childhood of Jesus (sometimes those portrayals are a bit sentimental) or to the tortured Christ on Golgotha, with Jesus on the crucifix bearing the crown of thorns and with his pierced heart (the "Sacred Heart"). Just mentioning the names of Georges Rouault (1871–1958) and Arcabas, whose given name was Jean-Marie Pirot (1926–2018), is enough to demonstrate the continuing enthusiasm for portraying the figure of Jesus Christ right up to today in painting, stained glass, sculpture, and precious metals.

Everything that has just been said stresses the continuity between Jesus and what he started. Nonetheless twenty centuries separate us from this historic figure! Are there ways for people of our time to have access to him? And in that case, is it possible to have access even apart from the path of the Christian faith?

We cannot ignore this "terrible abyss" that the philosopher and dramatist Gotthold Ephraim Lessing (1729–81) described, although closer to our own time the Danish philosopher and theologian Søren Kierkegaard (1813–55) could speak about a true possibility of contemporaneity with Jesus.

What can we think about relics of the passion of Jesus? For example, what about the crown of thorns that Saint Louis is said to have brought back from a Crusade to the Holy Land? He built the Sainte-Chapelle in Paris to house it. Then there is the wood of the True Cross that Saint Helena is said to have identified during excavations of Golgotha in the fourth century. Or again, there is the Sacred Shroud of Turin that bears the image of what is said to be the body of the crucified Lord; it is revealed occasionally to allow pilgrims "to encounter" Jesus. We are not obliged to treat these objects *automatically* as suspect or overrated. We might well be inclined to treat them with all the respect that a very long tradition of venerating them invites us to do. Nonetheless, we have to recognize that even with them we are still a very long way from this man who "died and was buried, rose again from the dead, ascended into heaven and is seated at the right hand of the Father," as we profess in the Creed!

We might recall here the gospel account itself: the disciples may have seen the empty tomb and the folded linens that had wrapped the body of Jesus, "but they did not see *him*" (Luke 24:24). Yet the question remains before us: By what means do we really hope to have access to him, or to encounter him?

We have already mentioned the contribution of the *historical-critical method* and the important results of that research in allowing access to him. Those results seem quite considerable in allowing us to affirm Jesus's existence, his teaching, his behavior, and his destiny, but also the way in which his eyewitnesses encountered, understood, and proclaimed him. This is especially impressive if we compare these elements with what we know with certainty about the philosopher Socrates or Gautama the Buddha.

But you must admit that such access or contact is indirect! As in the case of any personage of the distant past, a collection of knowledge about the person can never be equivalent to the lived experience of a face-to-face encounter!

Obviously, I cannot deny what you have just said! But I want to underline the following. With all we have said so far, we have not yet said everything about the possibility of a relationship or contact with Jesus today. In fact, we can always enter a second type of relationship with "the real Jesus." We can do so by reflecting on and living existentially the values and ideals, the rules of life, and the general understanding of human existence that he planted in the field of our civilization.

Life is a gift before which we should at least stand in wonder. Every person deserves our respect and concern. The little ones, the poor, the sick, and prisoners have a privileged right to our companionship and support. All those who are overlooked, forgotten, and rejected should be considered and placed in front. Even the enemy should be loved in some way. Pardon should be granted "seventy-seven times" (Matt 18:22). Evil may be in the human heart, but despite everything, its departure is always possible. Hope never dies. True happiness is in giving and in giving of oneself. The only true greatness and honor is in serving, not in being served, and so on. Trying to live by all these values and principles and putting them into practice can really put us into contact with Jesus, because all of that comes from him, at least in our culture and civilization. And we don't even have to become Christians to recognize it.

Assuredly, many sages, prophets, moralists, and humanists have been able to teach and live by a certain number of these values. Jesus certainly learned a number of these ideals from his Jewish tradition. But the problem is not that one or another of these values can be found in one author or another, in one movement or another, in one era or another, in one tradition or another. Therefore, other figures besides Jesus can enlighten us and have something to teach us. What counts is that all of this is found at the same time with Jesus. It has been effectively transmitted to us from him. And it is always accessible to us if we follow him, remain with him, and walk in his footsteps.

But you said that Jesus did not just bring us moral teaching. Those who recognized and still recognize him as the Christ affirm that he opened to the human race a/the way to salvation! How do those who believe in him see this other type of access to Jesus and relation to him?

Another way is also offered to those who are looking for an encounter with Jesus. It is what we call the way of the sacraments of the Church. Catholic Christians do not just affirm that God is so well disposed toward them that he simply expected to give them access one day to immortal life in his presence. They profess that by faith and their baptism, which plunges them ritually into the death and resurrection of Jesus the Christ, they become "(adopted) children of God." They can therefore also address him and entrust themselves to him as their Father. They do not just believe that God will refuse to consider their faults; they profess rather that in the sacramental celebration of pardon their sins are "destroyed/abolished" (see Heb 9:26). They do not just believe that God cares about them and watches over them. They believe that in the eucharistic celebration of the bread and wine, they have communion with the very life of Jesus the Christ, who has already conquered death and all forms of evil.

Obviously, no one is obliged to believe all that. And it is equally evident that only a passage through sincere confidence and faith can permit adherence to that message. But those who have effectively decided to "follow" Jesus Christ honestly feel able to say that they have had the experience of encountering him not just as a prestigious figure of the past who has already brought them many gifts, but as a *living person*. He is so living in fact that Paul—followed by many others—felt that he could declare: "For me, living is Christ" (Phil 1:21). In the end Christians have no other decisive reason to be Christians than this experience and conviction. For those who believe in the God who revealed and incarnated Jesus, faith is not an absurdity nor one more burden added to human existence but a light, a force, a happiness, a grace.

Will it be out of line or redundant for me to go on? I believe I can say that this is precisely what motivates Christian believers to overcome temptations to no longer be (or remain) Christian.[7]

Christianity is not the only religion in the human race to offer access to God, a way of living with moral values, and a path to salvation. To tell the truth, all the religions in the world believe that they were founded precisely to make proposals in these three areas. Doesn't that pose a problem for those who claim to represent Jesus Christ?

To the extent that it recognizes Jesus as the Christ, and therefore as the Messiah, the Christian religion can and must accept being challenged by other religions about this fundamental truth. It must moreover clarify its own positions and refine them in dialogue and debate. The question had already been asked of Jesus himself: "Are you the one who is to come, or are we to wait for another?" (Matt 11:3).

We must be realistic: Who is waiting for a Messiah today? Who is still waiting for *the* Messiah? Certainly, the language itself bears traces of some hope: don't we say that someone can be "awaited like the Messiah"? But we must acknowledge that hardly anyone really "believes in it." Most of the time we are conscious of putting all that in the category of the purely imaginary.

However, can we avoid wondering how this way of speaking continues to make sense among us: "a providential man," "a charismatic leader," "a savior of humankind," "Little Father of the peoples"?[8] The "messianic idea" had its day in the Soviet empire of the last century, as well as in both traditional and contemporary African cultures, with problematic results in every case.

That is certainly true, but in those cases, we are dealing with the political domain. What about the religious dimension? The question naturally arises first in the context of Judaism.

Obviously, it is in the religious domain that the figure of the Messiah and the notion of messianism still have meaning. In this domain, both are actively cultivated by the Jewish faith and nourished by reading the prophets of Israel. Those authors announce the coming of the "King-Messiah" at the end of time. This figure sent by the Most High God is to appear "on the clouds of heaven" as the supreme Judge of all the peoples and as the sovereign Savior of the righteous beneficiaries of his covenant. The convergence between believing Jews and confessing Christians is evident: both groups in the end are identified in relation to the Christ-Messiah. Nonetheless, they differ clearly in that the Jewish people believe that this Messiah will appear only at the end of human history (in fact, his arrival will even bring about that end). Christians, however, believe that "at the appointed time" he has already appeared in Jesus Christ in the heart of history and under the figure of one crucified.

We are presented with two different visions of the figure of the Messiah. The Jewish vision sees the Messiah as the one who will bring salvation to human beings and manifest to the world his divine glory by bringing to completion *at the end of the world* a history that he alone would have seen and directed "from the heavens above." The Christian vision says that he has already come in the course of human history to share human suffering and death in order to vanquish these evils on their own terrain. The central and crucial question is the following. Which vision of the Messiah seems more credible?

Paul, a Jew who became a disciple of Jesus the Christ, clearly came down on the side of a "crucified Messiah." He did it, we must say it once again, in the awareness that this could *only* represent a "stumbling block" for Jewish believers, and "foolishness" for Gentiles (1 Cor 1:23).

All we can do here is return to what was said earlier about the Christian understanding of the cross of Christ as God's revelation. However, it is possible to add that there are Jews who believe that, if they cannot as Jews admit that the man of Nazareth could be the Messiah, when the Messiah does appear at the end—a belief they share with Christians—perhaps at that time they may be able to discover that he had already come in Jesus.

And what about other religions? How do things look with them?

There is a lot to say on the objective, the spirit, and the conditions for dialogue between Christianity and the other religions. I am still speaking about the question of messianism as we have already introduced it. Considering Christianity's essential character, it is obvious that we can only consider religions confessing that there is only one God, or at least one transcendent Reality. That God or Reality decided to send to humanity an envoy presenting himself as his messenger, his representative, and his authorized delegate. In short, he is a mediator capable of bearing a message of salvation, and better yet, accomplishing true salvation. Posing the question in this way orients us toward what in the history of religions are called "religions with a historical founder." If we leave aside sectarian phenomena, there is, of course, Judaism (with its founding father, Moses), which we have already just treated. In addition, there are two other great religions in this category: Buddhism and Islam.

Buddhism owes its origins to the prince Gautama who lived in the north of India five centuries before Jesus Christ. He was recognized as the Buddha ("the enlightened one"), who opened to all his disciples the way of illumination leading to the supreme outcome in nirvana. But Gautama the Buddha is not a divine figure. His religion does not know in any way a unique, personal, and transcendent God, capable of giving himself a human mediation in history.

On its side, if Islam believes in God and in one God who chose in Muhammad a human envoy charged with revealing him, it is clear that, for him, Allah alone is God and Muhammad is only "his Prophet." From the Muslim point of view, that is enough to assure this Prophet his unique excellence. He came after Jesus (himself a prophet who should be venerated as such, as the Qur'an tells us) but Muhammad surpasses him definitively because, for Muslims, Muhammad marks the unsurpassable historical summit of God's revelation. But Muhammad is clearly not God, and a Muslim is too preoccupied with the question of monotheism to even consider the possibility that God could have a Son!

The response to the question posed at this point in our inquiry is therefore clear. Among the world religions that profess a revelation of God by a mediator/prophet/qualified representative, it is particular and unique to Christianity to announce that its agent of revelation reveals God *while being God himself*. God *incarnate*, Christians clearly affirm, most assuredly God—and *Son* of God. He is "*true* God born of true God," as the Nicene-Constantinopolitan Creed professes him. Personally, I would be inclined to say that both the specificity and the interest of Christianity stem from the fact that he, Jesus the Christ, is not only God and man, but that he has revealed himself as both divinely man and humanly God. Of course, we have to clarify this to remove any ambiguity. No difference, however striking it may be, can be sufficient to guarantee credibility, let alone superiority (if that term has any meaning here)! To stay with the question and answer format adopted throughout this book, I would gladly say that the right question here is: Regarding what and why, from what point of view, to what extent, and under what conditions does the Christian difference make "sense"?

Is it not appropriate to bring this dialogue about Jesus Christ to a close by explaining what the ultimate affirmation of the

Christian faith is, the one that refers to "Christ's return"? What do we mean when we mention such a return? Moreover, are today's Christians still waiting for it?

We should not forget that Jesus appeared in a historical context where messianic hope was particularly strong. Many prophets and charismatic personalities believed they were authorized to announce the coming of the last days and therefore the end of history. That in turn would bring the fulfillment of Israel's hope. Here we can recall discourses in the Synoptic Gospels where Jesus speaks about the end of time: "They will say to you, 'Look there!' or 'Look here!' Do not go, do not set off in pursuit" (Luke 17:23). Besides, had Jesus not announced from the time that he started preaching, "The kingdom of God has come near" (Mark 1:15)? Given its significance in the context of his time, how did his self-designation as Son of Man call to mind for his listeners the hoped-for figure "on the clouds of heaven" at "the End of Time"?

His disciples were still hoping, at the time of his departure, that he "was the one to redeem Israel." In the first letters during the years from AD 50 to 60, Paul's correspondents in Thessalonica had become a little anxious about this end-time. He tells them it will mark the Parousia:[9] that is, the return of the Lord. Toward the end of the first century, the apocalyptic currents were so prevalent that the last book of the New Testament, called the "Apocalypse of Saint John" also known as the Book of Revelation, remains constantly permeated with this mentality.

But Jesus came, and the end of time has not taken place...

That is obvious, and during the first two or three Christian generations, they had a hard time understanding the way in which God, in and with Jesus, could have answered the hope he had nurtured in his people. If he had truly come in Jesus, did they have to understand that it was in order to bring his people with him into eternal life in the short term? Or had he come to accompany them on their journey in the world through a history called to continue advancing toward its ultimate fulfillment "which only God knows"? This is the way the Second Vatican Council speaks of it. In other words, he was to remain with them from that moment on, "to the end of the age" (Matt 28:20; these are the last words of the first Synoptic Gospel) when all will be fulfilled.

The Christians had to admit, at least after a certain time, that the end-time would be accomplished in a different way. While waiting, they would have to get organized in order to last through the interim. They would also have to commit themselves to live in such a way that they could actually be counted among the beneficiaries of salvation when it would eventually be accomplished for them. In other words, as apocalyptic as the vision of the end-time was at the beginning, this dominant Christian mentality evolved more and more, so to speak, into an organizational-ecclesial and ethical-moral representation. Yet Christians never lost sight of and concern for "the end"!

After all, the Christians of the early days could not disregard what was likely awaiting them sooner or later both in their personal existence and at the end of the entire story of humanity. Jesus had opened a way and offered a happiness capable of vanquishing death. What, therefore, could their hope and their faith be from that time onward? And consequently, what can be the expectations for ourselves as their successors? This is where "waiting for Christ's return" finds its meaning.

Therefore, do Christians believe that Christ's return will come at the end of time?

It seems to me that the best way to deal with this immense question (somewhat overlooked by Christians themselves), is to refer to the presentation we find in the New Testament (Matt 25:31–46). This is how Jesus speaks of it:

> When the Son of Man comes in his glory, and all the angels with him, then he will sit on the throne of his glory. All the nations will be gathered before him, and he will separate people one from another as a shepherd separates the sheep from the goats, and he will put the sheep at his right hand and the goats at the left. Then the king will say to those at his right hand, "Come, you that are blessed by my Father, inherit the kingdom prepared for you from the foundation of the world; for I was hungry and you gave me food, I was thirsty and you gave me something to drink, I was a stranger and you welcomed me, I was naked and you gave me clothing, I was sick and you took care of me, I was in prison and you visited me." Then the righteous will answer him, "Lord, when was it that we saw you hungry and gave you food, or thirsty and gave you something to drink? And when was it that we saw you a stranger and welcomed you, or naked and gave you clothing? And when was it that we saw you sick or in prison and visited you?" And the king will answer them, "Truly I tell you, just as you did it to one of the least of these who are members of my family, you did it to me." Then he will say to those at his left hand, "You that are accursed, depart from me into the eternal fire prepared for the devil and his angels; for I was hungry and you gave me no food, I was thirsty and you gave me nothing to drink, I was a stranger and you did not welcome me, naked and you did not give

> me clothing, sick and in prison and you did not visit me." Then they also will answer, "Lord, when was it that we saw you hungry or thirsty or a stranger or naked or sick or in prison, and did not take care of you?" Then he will answer them, "Truly I tell you, just as you did not do it to one of the least of these, you did not do it to me." And these will go away into eternal punishment, but the righteous into eternal life.

How can we understand such a powerfully evocative text? It is a description of Christ's return. Now we are told right away that the protagonist is the one who was revealed and recognized in Jesus, namely this "Son of Man" who is God's "own Son." In the course of history, he came in the person of the Man of Nazareth.

But we are further told in the first place that this new "coming," this return, will occur at the end of history. This second coming will effectively mark that end. And then, it will be presented as neither more nor less than the judgment of history, of the entire history of humanity. In short, it is truly about the "Last Judgment," which sends us back one more time to the Christian Creed: "He will come again in glory to judge the living and the dead, and his kingdom will have no end."

This Judgment is presented as a decisive separation of good and evil, because some are treated by their Judge as "those blessed by my Father," while the others are condemned to "eternal punishment." Obviously, we can hardly avoid here a first reaction of reticence, or indignation, or even rejection: What? Can this be the "kingdom" and the "salvation" promised by the God of love and mercy[10] who sent his own Son precisely in order to offer these gifts to humanity?

Above all, it is essential to recall that the criteria for the separation at work here and for the judgment delivered are not of an institutional nature (what church or religion did you belong to?), nor of an ideological kind (what was your "vision of the world" or your personal opinion on one or another of the great questions in life?), nor even of a doctrinal type (do you believe in God and/or in eternal life?). There is only one criterion and it decides everything: How did you behave in relation to the one who was deprived of recognition and love, especially the little ones, the weak and the poor, the sick, the hungry, and the prisoner. Moreover, it is also very significant that this criterion is put in place and applied by a judge who is neither a potentate nor a torturer. On the contrary, he wants people to know that he himself is the one who was turned away and/or abused in the person of the little, the poor, the sick, and the like, for these are "his brothers."

What an astonishing judge, a unique royalty, a disconcerting power, a paradoxical glory: all that people associate with these terms, all that so strongly motivated and guided people throughout history, is turned upside down and rejected, when time comes to an end. When the time comes for judging the world, the criterion for judging everything, definitively and forever, will be what we have done to (and done for) "the least of [his] brothers [and sisters]"! Would it be better to say that, in the end, "what will count" above all and will "save" all is the love we will have shown in acts and in deeds for those who were deprived of it?

And the evangelical proclamation stresses that those who will come to trial will not be "trapped," since the message given is strictly the same as the one announced by Jesus, who is said to return at the end of time. It is a message that he himself put into practice throughout the time of his first coming. Because of the proclamation and realization of that message, he was put to death, and his resurrection from among the dead ultimately confirmed that message!

We know enough now to conclude our final question. Logically, it concerns the return of Christ at the end of history, and it sends us back to the last point we examined in offering to explain our understanding of Jesus. The great scene of the Last Judgment in Matthew's Gospel does not pretend to give us any detailed information that would allow us to describe the scenario of the end of the world. It does, however, enlighten us about what is essential—the one thing necessary.

Such is indeed the clear intention of the entire scene: it only wants to bring us back to the heart of the evangelical teaching and practice of Jesus the Christ. What counts in life, at least when we agree to understand it in the light of Jesus, is above all to extend love and render service to our brothers and sisters in the human family, beginning with the most deprived among them; and to believe the message of Jesus in Matthew's Gospel, even though we may not have recognized in those people the face of the Son of Man, the crucified one of Golgotha who became the risen one of Easter morning. We are nevertheless justified in hoping to be counted among those who, even if this comes as a surprise, will have the joy of being told: "Come, you that are blessed by my Father"! The only ultimate criterion: the way in which you will have loved your brothers and sisters.

I dare to close in this way:

≈ Everything leads the man and believing Christian that I am to think that this wonderful word would finally be understood, as Revelation says, by an immense crowd "from every tribe and language and people and nation" (5:9). On my part it is neither inconsistency nor condescension but a logical continuation of what I can understand about the God who has revealed himself in Jesus Christ. Not only does he want "everyone to be saved" (1 Tim 2:4), but he loves even "the unrighteous" (Matt 5:45).

≈ I can only rejoice that this high point of faith in Jesus the Christ brings us back to humanity and puts us at the center of the whole human "cause," starting with the most deprived among us. Pretending to offer worship to God without loving one's neighbor makes one "a liar." It would be to deceive oneself totally and, in the end, it would be "to lose one's life." But please allow me to address the following question to those who think they cannot believe in God. Can they not find in this belief a much stronger reason to love their brothers and sisters in this world?

CONCLUSION

"To Explain Jesus." That is the task I accepted at the invitation of the Éditions du Seuil publishing house. This book takes its place in a series of works. However, I must admit that I was confronted right from the beginning with an important question: Can Jesus ever really be explained?

"TO EXPLAIN IN ORDER TO UNDERSTAND BETTER."

We know that when it comes to human beings, explanations will not take us all the way to clarity. An argumentative or demonstrative type of explanation has little power when it comes to leading or helping others either to hope, to love, or to believe (in the sense of "trusting"). But these are precisely the attitudes that Jesus calls people to adopt, including vis-à-vis himself. And he clearly foresees that what he did, does, and is will remain at least largely problematic and perhaps entirely uninteresting for many people. When questions of human existence are at stake, our commitment to it and the meaning we can give to it will not be revealed by launching into grand explanations and multiplying them; and this is precisely what is at stake with Jesus. That is not how we will come into the light and lead others to it.

However, there is no possibility of hoping or loving, of trusting or believing without having reasons to do so; and this requires reflection. The mind has a role to play in this issue.

Current philosophical approaches to the science of interpretation can be very helpful to us. That discipline teaches us that when reflection is directed toward "human matters," it should not operate exclusively in the field of explanation. It should rather work at "understanding." More precisely, it teaches us that while explaining is important and even necessary, its true task is to work at offering a better understanding, as the French philosopher Paul Ricoeur tells us. In this case, the golden rule would be: "To explain more in order to understand better." Or even: "Never explain except to understand better."

To understand better! Therefore, we must accept that explaining can be helpful only if it is operating based on a prior understanding. Therefore, we speak currently about "pre-comprehension." If we can go along with this proposal, the true question we must pose is purely and simply to know what pre-comprehension, what prior understanding, is at work when we are trying to explain Jesus!

"EXPLAINING JESUS MORE," IN ORDER "TO UNDERSTAND HUMAN EXISTENCE BETTER."

The answer is simple. A certain number of those who claim to follow Jesus have lost sight of it; and it is hardly perceptible to many who are strangers to Jesus or have turned away from him. The pre-understanding in question concerns *human existence as such*. We should clarify this: it is about the understanding that everyone can have (and even must strive to have) of his or her own life. What enables people to go on living and what gives meaning to their lives?

Have you ever noticed that in the Gospels Jesus asks the question "Who am I?" He clarifies it in two ways: (1) He notifies those he is addressing that it is up to them to decide: he says, "*For you*, who am I?" (2) Prior to that question concerning himself, he invites them to pose the same question about themselves: "*And you*, what do *you* say?" This second question (which he poses before the one about himself) *concerns those who want to know who Jesus is*. The question "*You*, what do *you* say?" really means "Where are you in relation to the course of your life?" and how do you understand the "meaning of human existence"?

Jesus invites anyone who is curious to know about his existence to seek that knowledge in relation to his or her own existence and the meaning each one may already have given to it. Some may think that (1) they should begin with a question about God. (2) They would seek some sort of (positive or negative) "knowledge" about the deity. (3) Subsequently, they would try to verify whether that "knowledge" applies to Jesus. (4) Finally, they would take a step further and ask if it applies to God. This is *not* the way to proceed. The more useful way of going about the task would pass through the following steps: (1) Start with questions about myself; I almost certainly have raised such questions at some point in my life. What can I say about my own existence? What do I understand about myself? (2) Then, only after completing that task, I can ask the following question. Does the "knowledge" or understanding I have about Jesus help me find a deeper understanding of my own existence? Does it help me give more and better meaning and direction to my own life?

THE METHODOLOGY AND PROBLEMATIC OF THIS WORK

At this point the reader may be asking if the method I have used in this book is simply the invention of a modern or postmodern theologian. They may wonder if I have been drawn into the generalized secularization of the present age, if I am returning to all the idealism of the past, and if I am ultimately interested only in the "man" Jesus. On the contrary, I think the way I have undertaken my reflection about Jesus flows directly from his own attitude, considering what we know about that attitude. Contrary to much of what has been suggested in recent times, we have indeed seen that we know a great deal about that subject.

But the type of reflection applied here also draws on God's own attitude, at least if we believe what Jesus says about him and what Christian faith proposes about him. After very long historical preparations, when God wanted to make himself fully known to human beings, when he wanted to *reveal* himself completely to them, he chose to become man himself, taking flesh of the Virgin Mary. "He was incarnate of the Virgin Mary and became man," as we profess in the Christian Creed.

Considering what we now know about Jesus, this means that it is only in being truly and fully human that he could manifest and make us understand that he was God/the Son of God. Being truly and fully human necessarily includes dying. But this also means that we should never relativize, much less despise, our own human existence. I am invited to consider that Jesus may really have something to do with what we call God. Therefore, I must take seriously the understanding I already have about what it means to be "human."

As a theologian, as a believer, and as a pastor, I have often said that ultimately (to the extent that he exists) "God" can only be a great, truly a very great, mystery. Therefore, at least according to what I have learned and have come to know about Jesus, the true way to him must pass through the "mystery" that every human being is to him or herself. I am convinced that everyone strives to understand this mystery better in order to live a better life as a human being. In any case, this has been the question guiding my reflection in attempting to "explain Jesus."

A POWERFUL CONTEMPORARY WITNESS: DIETRICH BONHOEFFER (1906–1945)

The time has come for me to take leave of my reader. I can think of no better way to conclude than by citing a passage from the works of a believer, pastor, and theologian: Dietrich Bonhoeffer.[1] His *critical* reflection and his *confessing* witness have had a profound effect on me. He found meaningful and valuable knowledge about Jesus only to the extent that he came to a better understanding of his own human existence. This he did in dealing with the radical questions confronting him in Hitler's prisons. There he died for his resistance to the Nazi barbarity, the total inhumanity that the Nazi ideology represented. However, recent evolutions in our society show us that the womb that gave birth to that ideology unfortunately remains fertile. I conclude this study with his words:

> Matthew 8:17 makes it quite clear that Christ helps us, not by virtue of his omnipotence, but by virtue of his weakness and suffering. Here is the decisive difference between Christianity and all religions. Man's religiosity makes him look in his distress to the power of God in the world: *God is the deus ex machina*. The Bible directs man to God's powerlessness and suffering; only the suffering God can help. To that extent we may say that the development towards the world's coming of age outlined above, which has done away with a false conception of God, opens up a way of seeing the God of the Bible, who wins power and space in the world by his weakness. This will probably be the starting-point for our "secular interpretation."
>
> If the earth has been rendered worthy of bearing the man Jesus Christ, if a man like Jesus could

live there, then life is worth living for us as well. If Jesus had not lived, then our life, in spite of all the other people we have known, venerated and loved, would be deprived of meaning.

And if illusion has so much power in people's lives that it can keep life moving, how great a power there is in a hope that is based on certainty, and how invincible a life with such a hope is. "Christ our hope"—this Pauline formula is the strength of our lives.

We must always continue, very slowly and very calmly to immerse ourselves in the life, the word, the action, the suffering and the death of Jesus, in order to know what God promises and what he accomplishes. We have the assurance that we can always live in the proximity and presence of God and that life for us is an entirely new life; that nothing is any longer impossible for us, because nothing is impossible for God; that no earthly power can reach us without God's willing it; and that danger and distress only draw us closer to him. We are assured that we have no right to anything and yet that we can ask for everything; we are assured that in all this we find ourselves in a community that supports us. To all that God in Jesus has said a Yes and an Amen. This Yes and this Amen are the solid ground on which we stand.

NOTES

PREFACE

1. Remember that in our civilization, at least, we number our years beginning precisely from the presumed date of the birth of Jesus.

CHAPTER 1. HISTORY

1. *Canon* is the Greek term for "rule." The New Testament consists of the four Gospels (Matthew, Mark, Luke, and John), followed by the Acts of the Apostles, then the Letters of Paul and several others, and finally the Book of Revelation, attributed to Saint John.

2. *Gnostic* is derived from a Greek verb meaning "to know." It is a movement of religious philosophy combining Judaism, Christianity, and Oriental traditions that was widely spread in the first centuries of our era. It claimed to furnish its followers with secret divine knowledge that would assure salvation to those who had been initiated into it.

3. Rabbinic Judaism is the organization of the Jewish religion around the rabbis who guided and directed the Jewish communities. They were not priests but rather masters or leaders of the school teaching the Torah, that is, the Law. The Mishna is a compilation dating to the second century after Christ; the Talmuds (of Jerusalem and of Babylon) offer additional authorized commentaries.

4. This is a monumental work of historical research on Jesus, published in five volumes by Yale University Press in New Haven, Connecticut.

5. This is especially the case regarding the *Jerusalem Bible* (New York: Doubleday, 1966) and the *Traduction Oecuménique de la Bible* (Paris: Société biblique française/Cerf).

6. In Hebrew the Law of Moses is the Torah. For the Jews this word represents the first five books of the Bible. These books contain the Ten Commandments (or Decalogue), and the other prescriptions and rules whose observance alone will permit entrance into the "covenant" of life and salvation. These books record the founding events (from the Creation of the world to the return to the promised land by the exodus, the liberation from several centuries of captivity in Egypt).

7. See the last part of this book.

8. We will do this in the next chapter.

9. This celebration was and remains the annual commemoration of the liberation of the Jewish people from their captivity in Egypt (the exodus) by passing through the Red Sea under the leadership of Moses. According to John 18:28 and 19:14, the Jewish Passover ritual took place in that year in the night that followed the death of Jesus.

CHAPTER 2: MESSAGE

1. This expression is used by Jesus when two sisters receive him for a dinner. One of them, Mary, "sat at the Lord's feet and listened to what he was saying." The other one, Martha, "was distracted by her many tasks." She then lodged this complaint: "Lord, do you not care that my sister has left me to do all the work by myself? Tell her then to help me." But the Lord answered her, "Martha, Martha, you are worried and distracted by many things; there is need of only one thing" (Luke 10:39–42).

2. Or, the "Evangelical Discourse": Matt 5:1—7:28; cf. Luke 6:20–49. Matthew's intention is to present Jesus as the New Moses, bringing the "New Law," the charter of the "kingdom," and he proclaims its arrival.

3. In order to understand the meaning of this key word in the biblical and Christian vocabulary, we only need to refer to the

ordinary expression, "Thanks to you I...." Anyone can understand that the "I" in question could never have gotten out of the bad situation he or she was involved in by his or her own efforts. That person is indebted to a "you" who provided an opening or an escape.

4. Like "public sinners" (prostitutes and others), tax collectors and tax assessors were excluded from the community. They were sometimes guilty of certain unjust practices and also of collaborating with the occupying power.

5. Situated in the south of Palestine, Judea comprised Jerusalem and nearby Bethlehem. Its border with Samaria was about four kilometers north of Jerusalem. Galilee (which included Nazareth and the Lake of Tiberias, also known as the Sea of Galilee) was farther north.

6. Delivered from "seven demons" by Jesus (Luke 8:2–3), Mary Magdalene is present at the foot of the cross and at the burial of Jesus (Mark 15:47). According to John 20:11–18, she even received an "Easter appearance" of Jesus.

CHAPTER 3: IDENTITY

1. Toward the end of his Gospel, Luke recounts how two disciples of Jesus "were going to a village called Emmaus, about seven miles from Jerusalem, and talking with each other about all these things that had happened." They were grieving over the tragic end of the life of Jesus until Jesus catches up with them on the road "in person." Thus, they were granted one of his "apparitions" (24:13–35).

2. The "palms" referred to in this traditional expression were the palm fronds and branches that the crowds carried in joyful procession as they welcomed Jesus at his entrance into the Holy City.

3. *Messiah* is a noun derived from the Hebrew verb *mashah*, "to anoint." Remember that the kings of Israel were, like the priests, installed during rites that included as an essential element an anointing with oil.

4. Here I am drawing and summarizing from a different perspective something I said in another work of mine, *Être catholique aujourd'hui. Dans l'Église du pape François* (Paris: Bayard, 2014).

5. The expression *literary* here refers to a collection of data transmitted from one Christian community to another, at first orally and soon afterward committed to writing.

6. The word *salvation*, like the word *grace*, is another very important word in the Christian vocabulary. It is often considered difficult to understand and therefore is not much used today. There too we can refer to ordinary language usage. A child in catechism class said that one of his good friends was very sick and "no doubt lost." The catechist who told me this story asked, "What is the opposite of *lost*?" The response came back right away: "Well, *saved*, of course!"

7. This refers to the Christian rites called *sacraments* considered as permitting those who follow Jesus to enter communication with salvation and the life of God.

8. Another big word of the Christian faith: *mystery*. It is not a reality that would be inaccessible to human consciousness. Rather it "surpasses all understanding." Two consequences: (1) it can only be known if God himself takes the initiative in revealing it; (2) it is even greater when it is revealed than when it remains "hidden" (see Col 1:25–29). Blaise Pascal asserted that "man infinitely transcends man." His insight can help us discover that the Reality we are called to relate to can also go far beyond the idea we may already have of it.

CHAPTER 4: POSTERITY

1. Cf. Joseph Doré, *À cause de Jésus! Pourquoi je suis demeuré chrétien*, chap. 7 ("La rude expérience de l'histoire") (Paris: Plon, 2011).

2. In French, the two words *ministère* (ministry) and *métier* (job/profession) are etymologically related. Service is essentially included in the meaning of both of them.

3. Cf. above, chap. 1, n. 2.

4. These councils are called "ecumenical" because they were gatherings of bishops from the *oïkumēnē* (from the Greek word *oïkos*, meaning "house"); that is, from what they thought was the whole world.

5. A single exception is the case of the word *Filioque* (concerning the Holy Spirit who, in the Creed of the Church in the West proceeds from the Father *and the Son*). This word was added to the

Creed in the Latin rite and became the object of controversy with Eastern Orthodoxy.

6. "Scholastic theology," or theology of the schools, was the discipline taught at the universities, which were created in the thirteenth century. It was influenced by Aristotle's philosophy and sought to treat questions about God and religion in a scientific manner, applying principles to rational debates, "disputes," and argumentation.

7. Cf. Joseph Doré, *Être catholique aujourd'hui. Dans l'Église du pape François* and *Peut-on vraiment rester catholique?* (Paris: Bayard, 2012).

8. This expression was used for Tsar Nicholas of Russia and later of Stalin.

9. The Greek word *parousia* means "presence," "coming," or "return" when this coming follows a departure.

10. We should note the rich meaning of this beautiful word in the biblical and Christian vocabulary: *mercy*! In the background there is a Hebrew term that can be translated as "innards" or "insides." In the gospel story of the prodigal son the expression is translated in the following way: "He [the father] was filled with compassion." In Latin and the languages derived from it, the heart treats "misery" with "humanity." In German, the expression *Barmherzigkeit* relates the heart and the arms: for those who are unhappy and suffering in any way, it is a matter of opening one's arms to draw the suffering person close to one's heart.

CONCLUSION

1. The passages by the German Lutheran theologian cited here below can be found in Joseph Doré (ed.), *Jésus Christ et les chrétiens*, coll. "Jésus et Jésus Christ" (Paris: Desclée, 1981), 190–92. They can be found in the German work *Widerstand und Ergebung*, which appears in English under the title *Letters and Papers from Prison* (New York: Macmillan, 1972).